immaterial | ultramaterial

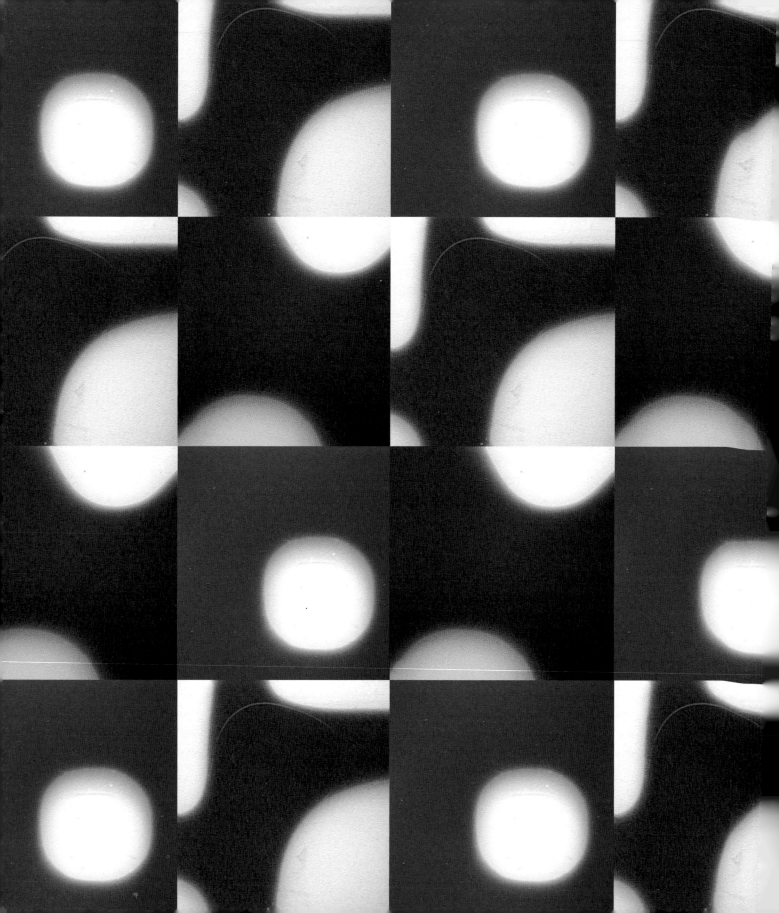

EDITED BY TOSHIKO MORI

immaterial | **ultramaterial**

architecture, design, and materials

HARVARD DESIGN SCHOOL
in association with
GEORGE BRAZILLER, PUBLISHER

George Braziller, Inc.
171 Madison Avenue
New York, NY 10016

ISBN 0-8076-1508-0

Printed in Hong Kong

Library of Congress Cataloging-in-Publication Data
Immaterial/ultramaterial: architecture, design, and materials /
edited by Toshiko Mori.
      p. cm. — (Millennium matters)
Includes bibliographical references and index.
   ISBN 0-8076-1508-0
1. Architecture and technology. 2. Building materials. I. Mori,
Toshiko, 1951- II. Series.
    NA2543.T43 I464 2002
    721'.0449—dc21
     2002006957

This is the second volume of a series of publications related to
the program Millennium Matters sponsored by the Department of
Architecture, Harvard Design School.

The Harvard Design School is a leading center for education,
information, and technical expertise on the built environment.
Its Departments of Architecture, Landscape Architecture, and
Urban Planning and Design offer master's and doctoral degree
programs and provide the foundation for the School's
Advanced Studies and Executive Education.

Jacket and book design by Matthew Monk, Providence, Rhode Island

contents

"Millennium Matters" refers to a program of events, sponsored by the Department of Architecture at Harvard University's Graduate School of Design during my tenure as department chair, which focuses on the relationships among materials, ideas, and design. The program has included exhibitions, symposia, lectures, and studios intended to orchestrate a dialogue that encompasses history, technology, and design.

One of its major components was a two-part exhibition dedicated to exploring the relationship of materials to the advancement of architecture. The first part took place in 2000 with an exhibition at the Fogg Art Museum, curated by Professor Christine Smith and Marjorie Cohn of the Fogg and titled "Before and After the End of Time: Architecture and the Year 1000." This exhibition and its accompanying catalog addressed the end of the first millennium and the revival of stone construction.

In the exhibition's second part, entitled "Immaterial/Ultramaterial" and led by Professor Toshiko Mori, we shifted the focus from the past to the future. This ambitious exhibition was produced by GSD faculty and students and explored what new materials suggest for the future of architecture. This volume presents the compelling if still highly speculative findings of the materials research that supported this exhibition. Its coverage includes varied perspectives on the development of new materials and techniques, the implications for the design process of these advances, and intriguing examples of built applications.

Thus it is the focus on this obstinate attribute of architecture—"materiality" —that links the intellectual content of the two programs. For materiality is more than a technical property of buildings: it is a precondition that promotes ideas, creativity, and pleasure in architecture, and it guides us to the loftiest aspirations of theory.

I regard this multilayered initiative as expressing the School's intense interest in the richly complex conditions that are repositioning architecture among cultural and technical practices in contemporary society. This book series and the related exhibitions are one expression of the GSD's continuous and broad interest in expanding our curriculum into professional, technical, and speculative areas of knowledge. With them we wish to present to the public the breadth of our academic endeavors in scholarship and artistic creativity.

JORGE SILVETTI
Nelson Robinson, Jr., Professor of Architecture

preface

The research that led to this publication and a related exhibition started in the spring of 2000 at the Harvard Design School as a seminar in advanced independent research. The work entailed a considerable amount of experimentation and had to allow for the possibility of mistakes and even outright failure as a necessary part of the learning process. The exploration had an unprecedented and unpredictable dimension, because no one had any premeditated idea about the product of our research. Unlike analytical and historical studies, our work involved thinking about things to come and speculating on the future potential of materials not yet widely available.

Many friends and colleagues contributed generously to this work, which was a genuine team effort. I would like first to thank Dean Peter Rowe of the Harvard Design School for his most crucial support. This project was initiated under the stewardship of Jorge Silvetti, chair of the department of architecture from 1995 to 2002; he has been an unwavering supporter and shared our belief that this effort will ultimately point out an important pedagogical direction for architecture.

I would also like to thank George Braziller, our copublisher, for taking on a book whose subject matter may not fit easily into any single category—a serious consideration in the business of publishing. Many others also believed in us and took a risk along with us to see what may lie beyond the safely defined horizon.

Some collaborators are specialists who contributed their talent, time, and resources: Dr. Steven Jones of Jet Propulsion Laboratory of the California Institute of Technology assisted us with aerogel research by generously donating aerogel material and a lab facility for production of the prototypes, as well as sharing with us his technical knowledge of the material. Professor Kurt Stallmann of the Harvard University Faculty of Arts and Sciences Department of Music collaborated with us on a sound installation in our exhibition, lending us the necessary equipment. He also organized many hours of valuable discussion between music students and Design School students. Ean White, the studio manager at the Harvard Studio for Electroacoustic Composition, contributed his engineering insight and knowledge not only to our exhibition but also to the ongoing discussion with our students about the relationship between space and sound. Shozo Toyohisa, a lighting artist and designer from Tokyo, demonstrated to us the virtues of energy-efficient and aesthetically beautiful fiber-optic lighting.

TOSHIKO MORI

acknowledgments

Many corporations from a range of industries donated materials and know-how to our research and fabrication. Asahi Glass Buildingwall Co., Optical Division, headed by Tetsuro Ikoma, donated fiber-optic lighting equipment for the duration of our exhibition. Toshio Suzuki and Yukio Hiraoka of Kilt Planning Office, along with Yasuki Hashimoto and Akane Nakabayashi of SGF Associates, assisted us with the design and installation of fiber-optic lighting systems.

The following individuals and companies donated materials and equipment for our research: Tatum Muchmore of Boston Felt Company, Fred Boulter of Boulter Plywood Cooperation, Roop Nagia of Dow Chemical Company, Katherine Ramsey of Dynamic Systems Inc., Jorg Manning of Eckart America LP, Sue Kintz of Foam Products Corporation, The Homasote Company, Jon DiGesú of Osram Sylvania Inc., Carlo Harkey of Phifer Wire Products, William Eskew of Quam-Nichols Company, Clay Western of Smooth-On Inc., Stan Townsend of Synair Corporation, Kathy Daniel of Synthetic Industries, and Russell Booth of Thermagraphic Measurements Inc. George Beylerian, founder of Material Connexion, has been a great resource and friend throughout our efforts. We are also extremely grateful for the support of Joseph B. Thomas (MArch '64) and Etel Thomas.

Design School students naturally played a vital role in the work. Tala Klinck coordinated the research and helped organize both the exhibition and the production of this volume. John May designed the website for the exhibition and research. The "Edge" team was comprised of Kristen Giannattasio, Heather Walls, John May, and Richard Lee, assisted by Mario d'Artista, Kyungen Kim, and Hyuck Rhee. "Surface" research team members were Bill Yen, Kristine Synnes, Dan Cheong, Jeremy Ficca, and Stephanie Granjacques. The "Substance" team was Billie Faircloth, Judith Hodge, Suzanne Kim, and Clover Lee, assisted by Yu-lin Chen. The "Phenomena" team was Tala Klinck, Kendall Doerr, Michael Meredith, Jinhee Park, Mette Aamodt, and Denise de Castro. Sound research and installation were the work of students from the Department of Music: Helen Lee, Peter Whincop, and Elliott Gyger. Throughout the spring of 2001, we sponsored roundtable discussions featuring a range of noteworthy visitors—architects, artists, material scientists, and writers; the proceedings of these sessions are selectively presented in this volume.

I would like to thank all authors for continuously exchanging fresh ideas on the subject of materiality in architecture. I also thank our publications editor, Melissa Vaughn, for offering intelligent editorial advice and keeping us on track as we worked on this complex and challenging volume. I appreciate the enthusiastic collaboration Matthew Monk provided in designing this beautiful book, which well reflects the exhilaration we felt throughout our process of conducting research, mounting an exhibition, and preparing material for publication.

But most of all, we were able to venture into new territories of inquiry precisely because of the Design School's open-minded atmosphere, which fosters fertile and dynamic intellectual exchange and experimentation. Jorge Silvetti deserves our heartfelt appreciation for making the School the most collegial and civilized academy of architecture. By encouraging different ideas and allowing varied points of view to emerge, he helped fuel an ongoing dialogue about the future direction of architecture.

Throughout history, a basic human desire to make things has prompted count-less innovations in methods of production. During the industrial revolution, a significant cultural discourse addressed the staggering impact of new tech-nologies on all reaches of society, including architectural production. In a similar spirit, at the Harvard Design School we thought the time was ripe to examine recent developments in digital technology and the resulting shift from mechanical modes of production.

The time frame assigned to architectural production has been continu-ally compressed, and the distance between design and fabrication is narrowing. At the same time, we are losing direct contact in both social inter-action and the material fabrication process. We have come to rely on various software programs, which assist us yet discourage critical awareness, as they are designed to solve problems easily and quickly; in so doing, however, they leave no room for discursive and speculative thinking. This loss of contact is reflected in our increased use of remote control and simulation techniques for exploring virtual reality. With a push of a button, it is easy to achieve the decep-tive appearance of design completion. This distance and disengagement prevents the architect from playing a responsible role as cohesive thinker, designer, and fabricator.

In addition, the division of labor since the industrial revolution continues to reflect increasing specialization, which has progressively dimin-ished the role of the architect, especially in the area of construction. This narrowing of responsibility has also led to architects being further subdivided into categories such as technical, artistic, and theoretical—preventing us from becoming a coherent voice in society.

A related issue is in the decline in architects' involvement with the study of material properties and research into fabrication processes. The research described in this volume can be rightfully characterized as a reaction against the recent proliferation of virtual modes of representation, where tech-nique is discussed only in terms of its visual representation. During the indus-trial revolution, the arts and crafts movement was characterized as a reactionary response. In our time, however, the world is not so clearly divided into proponents of machine-made goods, advocates of digitally processed arti-facts, and supporters of the handcrafts tradition. Our era is more nuanced, and our value systems are complex and varied. Our research aims to promote a greater understanding of materiality, tactility, and fabrication processes—not

TOSHIKO MORI

introduction

only to allow us to better employ traditional materials but also to embrace the possibilities presented by new materials.

In addition to considerations of traditional modes of mechanical and manual production, our research includes explorations of digital technologies such as CNC, CAD/CAM, stereo lithography, and three-dimensional printing, and concepts for mass customization and advanced performance-monitoring systems. Because the majority of digital processes are invisible, we sought to make our efforts visible and to demonstrate specific lines of inquiry by different teams of architects and students. Since there are other organizations that collect and archive building materials, we have focused instead on fostering creative study of materials and fabrication processes. We wanted to create a laboratory where divergent ways of thinking transform materials and ultimately empower our discipline to challenge the passive mode of material use.

Supporting this speculation, two distinct but related talents of architects—the power of observation, and the creative use of imagination—enable us to identify technological innovations and apply them to design activity. By understanding materials' basic properties, pushing their limits for greater performance, and at the same time being aware of their aesthetic values and psychological effects, an essential design role can be regained and expanded. This holistic approach to material investigation includes conceptual, theoretical, aesthetic, philosophical, performative, and technical issues for speculation.

As new materials are invented and technological advances made, architectural practice has moved from working within the limits of static materials to transforming them into dynamic elements by combining, laminating, casting, and weaving. We can vicariously experience the fantasy of immortality through technological innovation, as it is conceivable that we will soon be able to create invincible materials. We can theoretically produce materials to meet specific performative criteria; this transformation often takes place at the molecular level, where materiality is rendered invisible (such as in nanotechnology). Thus the sea change we sense is subtle and subversive because it is occurring below the surface of visible artifacts. We embraced the word "latency" to express our attitude toward envisioning the future, for we wish to acknowledge the reality both slightly above and just below the surface. The research presented here is latent because we do not provide clear answers; rather, we have identified a range of areas that offer promising potential for future exploration.

Historically speaking, the discovery and utilization of materials such as concrete and steel changed the course of architecture. In considering applications of new materials, we soon realized that research on innovative methods will have a profound impact on conventional design methodologies, general conceptions of form, and modes of production. Yet our intellectual and pedagogical challenge lies not in an episodic fascination with individual new materials but in the long-term direction that the project may assume. How will materiality respond to the infinite transformational processes of digital production? Internalization, invisibility, and speed of transformation demand from architects a nuanced understanding of materials and fabrication techniques, because production of materials and fabrication of building components will soon be simultaneous. The age of mechanical production, of linear processes and the strict division of labor, is rapidly collapsing around us.

We are now in an age where light, chemistry, and especially nanotechnology form the basis of manufacturing. Conventional manufacturing processes will nonetheless continue to exist, and may even result in function following or even conforming to form. Therefore the ethical debate about the correct use of materials and appropriateness of tectonic language or structure will also continue. Architects and other citizens must actively make choices about where to build, what to build, how to build, and with what to build.

For the purposes of our research, four faculty-led groups focused on the themes of "Edge" (with Nader Tehrani), "Surface" (with Marco Steinberg), "Substance" (with Ron Witte), and "Phenomena" (with Toshiko Mori). The four groups selected for study materials commonly used as substrate and valued for their performative qualities, such as engineered boards, thin plywood, rubber, foam, felt, and aerogel. In their strange and humble neutrality, these materials act as flexible media that go through various stages of mutation and fabrication to increase use, capacity, and performance. In addition, we recognized sensory components—light, sound, and smell—as materials. In between are coatings and paint—thin layers of application that optically and thermally change surfaces.

In our investigation, we were very careful to determine the safety of each material in various processing modes; we used protective equipment and worked in facilities capable of providing necessary ventilation and meeting other safety criteria. We also looked at the origins of various materials, their place in the economy, and the implications for their sustainability to understand the value system of materials in the world at large.

The "Edge" team focused its efforts on two methods of fabrication using ancient techniques of tailoring and casting to give shape and structure to thin and malleable materials such as plywood and clear rubber. These techniques are adaptable to both mechanical and digital production applications that extend far beyond their humble handcraft origins. Working with and against the nature of chosen materials, the team sought to extend the materials' spatial, tactile, and experiential potential through the employment of these imaginative techniques. This method previews developments in fabrication that will enable individual units to be something other than standardized, repeated modules. Both form and function can be defined by this ability to produce a variety of shapes while defining both continuity and discontinuity of material and its surface.

The "Surface" team also investigated tectonic, technical, and tactile permutations, systematically producing specimens of reuse and even misuse of engineered products. These homogenous, task-oriented materials are good at high-quantity applications, but lack the complexity and character of traditional materials. Yet the very qualities of anonymity and blandness were taken as positive attributes that allow transformative operations. Innovation in this research takes place through the role of the imagination, in asking what potentials we have not yet perceived in common materials. New uses are envisioned through reappropriation and recontextualization of materials for divergent purposes.

The "Substance" team presaged an age of gradient materials that are detailed at the level of microns, whose material character is transformed by chemistry, and whose surfaces are comprised of contours rather than an assembly of parts. The "Phenomena" group worked with materials that react and respond to heat, weight, sound, moisture, light, and touch. Included are immaterial elements such as light, sound, air, and smell that are integrated into the spatial configuration to signify boundaries and thresholds. Coatings, paints, and films are thin materials that act as additive media for performance enhancement; this group of materials is the prime candidate for further developments via nanotechnology. They are capable of transforming properties of the materials to which they are applied, potentially altering both appearance and performance.

During the spring of 2001, we sponsored a series of discussions about materials with colleagues and visitors to the Harvard Design School. Included in this volume are excerpts from these provocative sessions, which added numerous examples of material innovation in contemporary practice to our research-based speculations.

The reciprocal relationship between materials and humans is the basis of attachment and even obsession. From the appreciation of tactile materials to the experience of immaterial qualities registered through other human senses, the direction of research starts to move in the direction of psychology. Material is a universal language of culture and civilization. It is accessible and understandable to young and old. As an artifact, it carries with it many messages pertaining to: the place of its origin, the reason for its having been made, the history of its use, its mythical and cultural meaning, its performance value, its economic value, and its life cycle—including the possibility for recycling or eventual disposal. The study of material culture thus connects us to fundamental issues of humanity. The particular mindset necessary is one that scans, scavenges, and locates existing and imminent innovations in material technology that can be applied to the making of our environment. This opportunistic strategy is proposed to circumvent the twenty to twenty-five years that it normally takes to incorporate new materials and new technologies into architectural applications. Within the world of material research generally, architecture commands a small portion of resources and attention, because its use cycle is longer than that for most other manufactured products; further, it is not the major consumer of any individual material. Thus formal materials research must be combined with creative appropriation of advances made in nonarchitectural areas.

Civilization is in a precarious state now, filled with misery, destruction, and terror. Because of recent events, there is an urgent need for greater safety and better performance from buildings. Technology will continue to be stealthy (as opposed to overt) and dynamic (instead of static); yet if we are intelligent in our approach to integrating material and fabrication research into architecture, we can claim a larger territory of knowledge encompassing science, technology, and design. Then we can reaffirm the role of architects as constructors of civilization and continue to practice with confidence, pride, and generosity toward humankind.

edge

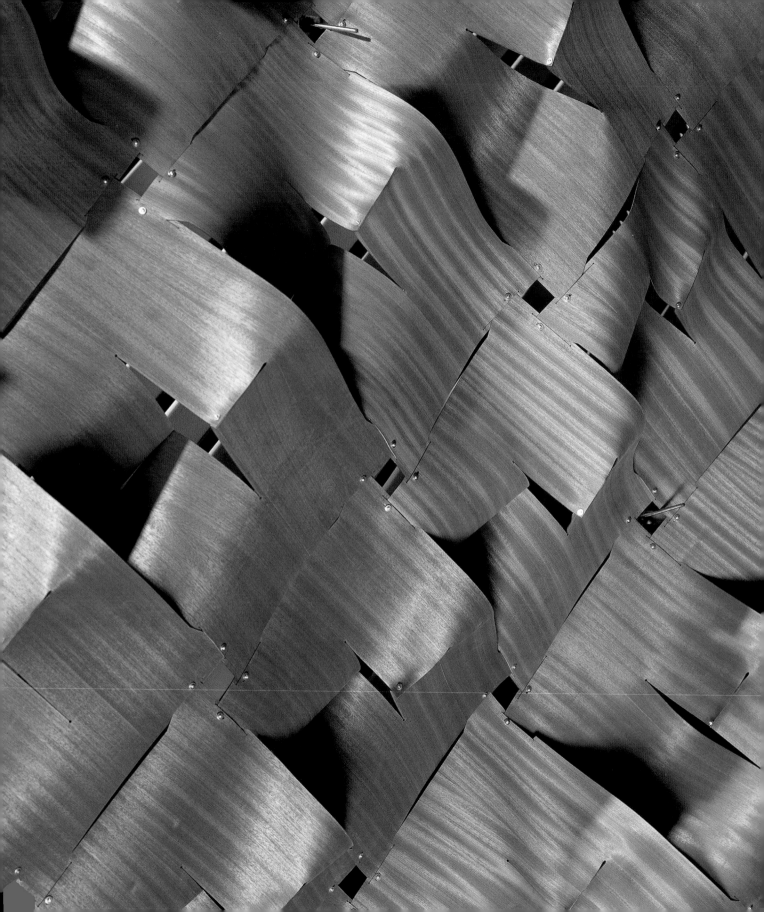

edge

NADER TEHRANI, KRISTEN GIANNATTASIO,
HEATHER WALLS, JOHN MAY, AND RICHARD LEE

New materials provide designers with significant possibilities for shaping space and fabricating with new methods, yet many opportunities for innovation exist within traditional materials as well. Thin plywood and rubber, for example, particularly lend themselves to reconsideration. Our experiments with these materials were guided by a set of questions, themes, and theoretical premises that help to contextualize our new work within broader architectural and historical debates. The areas of research include a study of material properties, historical precedents, the interface between geometry and materials, the problem of connections and material junctures, and a sample site analysis.

One exercise required the design of an enclosure, to address several mandates. First, the enclosure would be made of a single material using a consistent and systematic method of construction. Second, one would have to design three joints by the "turning" of three corners: the junction between a horizontal and vertical surface (floor to wall), the junction between two vertical surfaces, and finally the junction between a vertical surface and a horizontal surface (wall to ceiling/roof). Third, three types of apertures would be designed within the enclosure: one as a threshold, another for a view, and the third for the passage of light. Of course, the exercise is fraught with problems, as few materials can reasonably negotiate the tectonic mandates of floor, wall, and roof in a singular and consistent fashion—not to mention the addition of apertures of various sorts.

And yet therein lies the seduction of this exercise: the idea that the requirements of traditional tectonics may be challenged and indeed overcome through the invention of a new system of units. The aim then is to demonstrate the flexibility of a single medium when confronted with unconventional problems. Also latent within the exercise is the idea of overcoming the traditional linearity of the design process—designing the critical detail or juncture concurrent with the design of spatial and formal biases, essentially pointing to the potential reciprocity between the two scales.[1]

Metaphors, Operations, and History

Drawing from the historical link between architecture and textiles, we borrowed techniques from apparel design and tailoring to discover a new category of tectonic relationships. Working at once with and against the nature of specific materials, we attempted to radicalize the materials' spatial, tactile, and experiential potentials. Calibrating geometries and material conditions, we imported sartorial techniques to give syntactic and tailored precision to the various edges, seams, and connections of the prototype structures. The two prototypes simultaneously addressed architectural exigencies pertaining to structure, siting, program, and visuality. Working with wood, rubber, and screen-mesh rebar, we deployed techniques of pattern making, pleating, darting, and tabbing—among others—to provide structure and geometric precision.

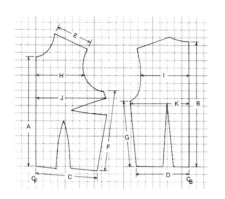

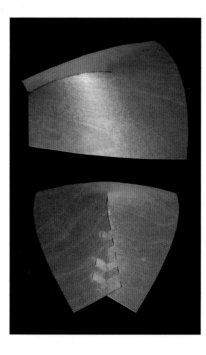

Reconsidering Plywood

In reassessing the applications of plywood, the challenge was to discover a technique for bending wood that did not rely on the methods developed by furniture makers of the early 1900s, which are still in use today. These methods, effective in mass-producing identical units, require a multistep process of mold making, cutting, laminating, and applying heat and high pressure. With the technology available today, we sought to develop a "dry" process of bending wood. This method, incorporating CAD-CAM technology, would also allow for the customization of mass-produced units.

A desire of furniture makers such as Thonet was to efficiently fabricate a chair from a single piece of wood. The solution transformed the planar material into a form through the specificity of the geometry or pattern cut from the wood. The form would materialize once the appropriate "limbs" were bent into position. This new method, akin to tailoring, relies on the transformation of a two-dimensional material into a three-dimensional form through incisions and reconnections. In apparel design, these incisions are called darts: material is removed from the fabric, and the incision is then sutured or seamed to create tailored curves to fit the body. The dart and cuff techniques were studied and applied to thin plywood sheets, resulting in various transformations.

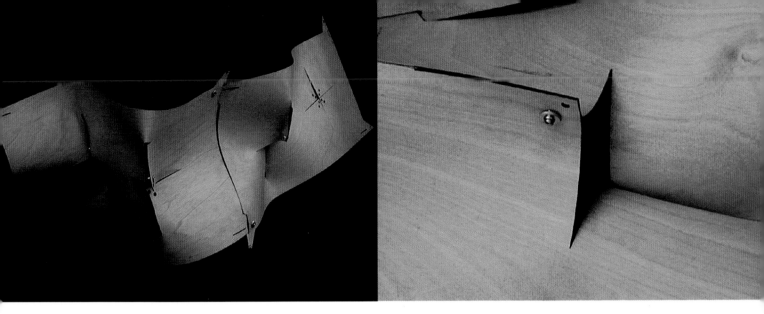

Design development began with a 3-D digital model of a space built in Rhinoceros, a computer-modeling program. The overall form of a wood membrane was developed and transformed in digital space simultaneous to the development of the real-world material and structural requirements. Views generated within the modeling program allowed the design team to quickly test many configurations and finally generate a form that would interact within specific conditions. In this case, a column was wrapped and an archway passage created. At the same time, materials were investigated and tested for their use in the overall form, and details were examined as a unit of construction was developed.

We designed a panel to allow for a small tolerance of slippage between the individual units, and also to permit an overall form with indefinite edges—a concept that allowed our prototype the possibility of being part of an extended system. Maximum unit size was determined by the given capacity of the laser cutter available, with each piece labeled and oriented as it was cut. The crosscuts and seams—the key to realizing the overall form—were developed using a 1/2 inch = 1 foot CAD-CAM model; the structure was fitted in the way that a dressmaker fits the human form.

Final construction began with the laser cutting of 192 individual panels of thin-ply sapele mahogany, with each piece cleaned and finished before being riveted into its own complex curvature. Each panel joined with the next in a four-way tab-and-slot system—the crucial moment of interface between the aggregation of individual units and the smooth geometry of the overall form. This moment also incorporates the structure that holds the entire form aloft: a bent aluminum "spider," which aligns with and is fastened to the hardware of the tab system. This "spider" allows for a connection with metal rods hanging from positions on the ceiling (determined by the original computer model); these rods can be glimpsed protruding into the intersection, both concealing and revealing the structure and connections of the structure.

This line of research focuses on the interface between problems of aggregation and geometry—aggregation referring to traditions of construction that involve the assembly of discrete units. When confronting problems of geometry and standardization, different strategies have emerged through history for the resolution of edges, corners, and junctions. Some strategies are related to the provision of allowances for the ease of construction, while others are directed toward the

definition of a particular linguistic attitude. Either way, any position defines a relative idea about architectural resolution. From the didactic permutations of corners by Mies van der Rohe to the open-ended formal experimentation of Frank Gehry, the notion of resolution remains as ubiquitous as the forms in which their architects are invested. Drawing from these two divergent traditions, our work attempted to create reciprocity between broader geometric problems and the units of construction. The prototype was conceived as a wood membrane whose geometry could accommodate—indeed radicalize—a variety of conditions. In turn, the units of construction were conceived systematically, with the possibility of calibrating different amounts of light, air, and sound through varied slits in the wood membrane. Able to address programmatic, structural, perceptual, and relational contingencies, the potentials of the syntax of parts were demonstrated by the material's flexibility and malleability.

A New Approach to Rubber

We next focused on the symbiotic relationship between compressive and tensile elements within the casting process. If conventional concrete construction involves a reciprocal relationship between poured concrete and reinforcement bars—with the rebar absorbing the tensile forces and the concrete aggregate taking on the compressive forces—the rebar is nonetheless seen as having a secondary role, remaining suppressed within the cast as a silent voice.

Traditionally, the art of casting has developed forms by exploiting the physical properties of a cast material. The most basic techniques involve the initial preparation of a liquid, which is then poured within a negative mold and allowed to cure. In casting, the relationship between the cast object and its physical structure is resolved by the phase properties of the material—quite literally, the molecular limit between solid and liquid.

More complex casting techniques have evolved over time. One specific example is reinforced concrete casting, arguably the dominant paradigm in the building industry. In this process the reinforcement bars are arranged as a dumb armature within the mold, entombed within the concrete as it cures in the formwork. As a final product, the concrete gives the impression of homogeneity because the reinforcement remains largely unseen, extending beyond the casting only at moments of concealed connection. The relationship between structure and surface is both a visual denial and a physical correspondence. In the initial stages of our research, it was imagined that perhaps this relationship could be inverted.

The beauty of most evolved casting techniques lies in both the sensitivity to the properties of the cast material and a pairing of those properties with an appropriate method (e.g., bronze casting is equal parts metallurgy and art). Recognizing this, we sought to develop two strains of research: one that merely examined the physical and phenomenal properties of our selected casting material, rubber, through exhaustive analysis, and a second investigation that speculated on ideal methods for casting the rubber with reinforcement. The first path essentially involved cataloging and classifying the results of numerous test casts (experimenting with various types of rubber, casting samples at different thicknesses to determine tensile properties and compressive strength, assessing effects of lighting, etc.); the second demanded that we find a material that could act as reinforcement without denying the two most salient qualities of the rubber itself: flexibility and translucency.

By adopting rubber as a material of research, we were able to capitalize on the material's translucency to display—moreover, exaggerate—the potentials of the reinforcement held within the cast, giving a thematic primacy to the tailoring of the membrane. By opting for PVC-coated fiberglass screen mesh over bars, we enabled the reinforcement membrane to be folded, pleated, cuffed, and twisted as a vehicle to create struc-

5

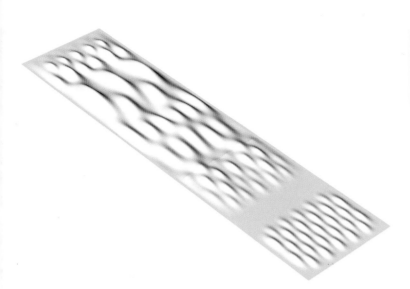

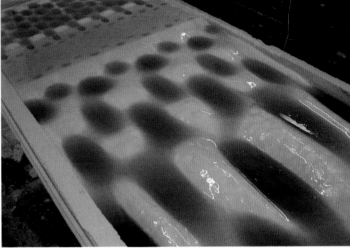

tural connections. The reinforcement membrane thus maintains a relative autonomy from the cast, extended outside of the cast to make necessary attachments.

We discovered that the mesh, when subjected to various formal techniques borrowed from fashion (pleating, folding, crimping, ironing, sewing), could be tailored with a degree of precision. The mesh "rebar," once tailored, with its movements detailed, could respond to the changing section of a cast-rubber piece. This was a crucial discovery, given that our early test castings revealed that the form of the rubber—that is, its final response to gravity—was primarily a function of its sectional thickness. Thin castings behaved similar to a fabric, while the thicker casts maintained their rigidity to a much greater degree. We found that the sectional variation could be calibrated along the length of an object, forcing a single piece to be thin and pliant at some points, while still thick and (comparatively) rigid at others. We began to realize the possibilities inherent in our new reinforced casting method—one in which both surface and structure could be precisely calibrated, all the while remaining, in their final states, flexible, translucent, and highly manipulable.

In the final stage, we focused on mold production. We again used Rhinoceros software to develop the final form of the cast-rubber panels. The molds were milled, using Master-CAM milling software, from thick foam on a CNC router bed. The section of the mold was developed to allow the final rubber castings to respond to conditions of the sample site (a wall and ceiling space, which could both serve as attaching surfaces, and a floor area). The mesh was tailored to respond to that changing section—at times working in concert with the undulating surface, at times opposing it.

The final pieces were hung at a distance from the back wall, each from two point connections at the ceiling, and pulled taut against the back wall near the floor. The thinnest section of the rubber casts generated natural curvature near the floor, finally splaying out into thicker "floor mats" that reached out into the room. Fiber-optic lighting highlighted the translucent amber color of the rubber. The inner mesh appeared as darker shadows cast deep within the pieces, its fine grid providing measure and definition to the uninterrupted exterior surface—simultaneously defining and dissolving the composition of object and structure.

Note

1. I developed this exercise initially for
the RISD core program in 1998. At the
same time, a studio taught by Kyna Leski,
"Systems and Units," was being conducted
at RISD, resulting in a fruitful dialogue
between the two studios. In the Leski
studio, the system was to be understood as
"a complex whole with an inherent logic
of functioning of form, geometry, material,
and structure. The system needed to be
continuous, expandable, and contractible.
The system was to be constructed out of
rigid material and needed to be disinte-
grated. As such, seams needed to be found,
cuts made, nodes and components identified." Their work is published in *RISD
Works* 1998.

ROUNDTABLE DISCUSSION *with mack scogin, merrill elam, sheila kennedy, and laurie hawkinson*

This discussion brought together four architects who take material innovation seriously, though they do not take a similar approach to process. In a conversation led by Toshiko Mori, they exchanged perspectives on how practice itself must change to support the creative use of new materials. In terms of material research and professional practice, we are facing a paradigm shift. These architects forge individual paths for their research and practice to cope with this uncertain yet exciting future direction for architects.

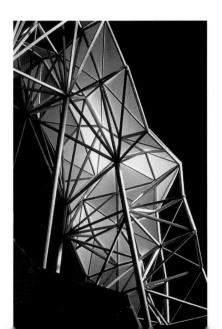

Toshiko Mori I have to make a few comments about Mack Scogin and Merrill Elam, as I have admired their work for many years. They describe the processes of practice as embedded in the tactility of architecture, and they extend practical discourse beyond simple use of specific materials. Rather, they use tactile and sensory materials and observe the extraordinary in the ordinary. They discover wonders in common materials —in terms of context, site, program, and in the tectonic—and that is what is so extraordinary about their work. We are used to theorizing architecture, using words to describe it, but their architectural language goes beyond the words they use—it is sensory and tactile: things are heavy or light, rough or smooth. We have often been deprived of this sort of language in recent discussion of architecture.

That's why their practice is exuberant and looks like so much fun— because for them architecture is about discovering something new every day. The humble way in which they describe their mode of operation as "anxious and guessing" shows how the process of discovering life fuses their lifestyle and practice.

Yet their practice is actually a sophisticated process of continuous analysis and synthesis, honed by thoroughly trained minds that engage both the senses and the intellect. Once you see their buildings, the experience goes beyond the brain. Cognition happens through the body, and that is what we all strive to achieve as architects. Their language of architecture is beyond explanation; it's visceral. And it enlarges the discourse of materiality beyond the simple application of concrete or steel.

Facing page: Mack Scogin Merrill Elam Architects, Clayton County Headquarters Library, Jonesboro, Georgia, 1988
Left: Mack Scogin Merrill Elam Architects, Atlanta Pavilion, Atlanta, Georgia, 1994

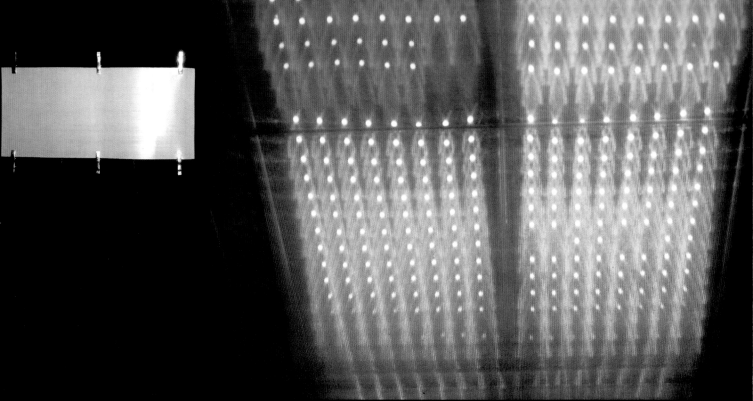

In many ways the practices of Laurie Hawkinson and Sheila Kennedy also engage with tactility; their work considers the marginal and the unusual, and discovers new relationships between object and site. They both have been active in rethinking the way we use traditional materials and in devising new ones.

Sheila Kennedy I would like to pose for discussion a material predicament that's captured the interest of my partner, Frano Violich, and myself. There is a new intensity in the integration of media and materials, a condition that began in the nineteenth century with the interest in conductivity, as electricity was first being understood in science and popular culture.

But certainly we are seeing, with nanostructures and solid-state technologies, the possibility of an even more integral relationship among the organization of light, information, thermal controls, and material properties. This creates an interesting situation for architects, producing all sorts of predicaments, as it calls into question many of the cultural values that we might associate with materials.

Mori In your practice, material sometimes precedes the project. . .

Mack Scogin That's one thing that is a little different in the way that we look at materials and the way Sheila does. We don't generate any material research, other than what comes out of a project—the project comes first. And most of the work we do in proposing new or slightly different materials is really just an alteration of existing systems. For example, we make a funny-shaped brick. And Merrill's big on painting buildings. (laughter)

Mori Your famous black brick. . .

Kennedy I think that's a great idea. It's simple things like that that allow architects to create new uses for materials. On a number of occasions, we've used materials that are normally used in one context in another—perhaps it is normally used on a roof and you simply use it on the side of the building.

Scogin In one case we wanted a building that had a lot of texture and depth to it. It's kind of a slick shape, but we wanted something on the shape that was not slick—that was quite rough and rusticated. We actually started out using slate —throwaway pieces from the slate quarry. When they quarry the slate

in big slabs, the end pieces are rough, and they cut those off and throw them away. But they're amazing shapes, and we were going to take that stuff and stack it just like stone. I don't know how to describe it—it's a very unusual pattern. (laughter) But it is that type of thing we do, in terms of our material research. I don't even think you would call it research; it's sort of—

Mori Necessity.

Scogin Necessity—material necessity, that's what it is. And we've done a lot of that, frankly, because most of our buildings are incredibly inexpensive, and we have to milk the architecture out of them somehow. (laughter) And, so Merrill paints corrugated metal—typical corrugated metal with a pattern on it.

Kennedy Inventing ways to make a building affordable is important; it's the difference sometimes between seeing ideas built or not.

In our practice we have begun a working group to focus on the design and research of new materials. This research is very exciting for us. The architectural imagination is well suited to take on interdisciplinary problems and coordinate strategies for idea production and fabrication in architecture. And sometimes—for example, with our Chameleon Cloth—you end up with a material so intriguing that it generates a project in your mind, an idea that you wouldn't have had if you didn't have prior contact with that material and its properties. So sometimes ideas about the material and its performance lead to the project.

Mori Laurie, can you talk to us about the fantastic ferry terminal—the first terminal built in New York harbor in how many years?

Laurie Hawkinson The Wall Street Ferry Terminal is the first terminal built in Manhattan in more than fifty years. Now there's this great impetus to support waterborne transit, because it is less expensive and can be done more quickly than building a subway.

Mori I call you "the industrial scavengers," because you appropriate different industrial building precedents and material uses for other buildings, producing the impression of amazingly large-scale buildings for smaller projects. You use inexpensive materials in normal production. But the size of the industrial buildings you use as a reference and how you use materials and detail in your new buildings give a sufficient scale to command a civic presence within Manhattan. How are you using industrial materials, and how do you scale them within the larger urban context?

Hawkinson A lot of what you are describing as "scavenging" is budget-driven. This is what Mack is saying —that often the budgets given to architects come from a hypothetical feasibility study. And, for instance, a new project might involve 200 million square feet for an office building, but with the low cost per square foot, all you can build is—what do they call it?— "plain vanilla." But whether a client's budget is $200 a square foot for a curtain wall or $800, we are always up against a budget. Working within these parameters pushes us—this is one way we got to certain industrial materials. We were trying to find materials that would actually hold up over time. Not being able to afford materials of higher quality, such as stainless steel, for instance, forced us to look for ways we could push not just the material but also its presence and how it might have an architectural effect in and on a building.

Mori It seems to me that the role of architecture was previously determined by working within a preestablished context; there was a certain means of innovation and operation. Or there are other kinds of limits embedded within materials—and by making things highly visible—perhaps it reduces the ability for them to be silent. What's the limit to which the visibility of something is actually reducing its ability to become part of the larger context? Are there other kinds of limitations on what one can do?

Kennedy That's a tough one. The dynamics of time can be engaged. The duration of light or information media allows the same surface to be silent and part of the background at times and materially present at other times. Such surfaces are like chameleons—their ability to change over time enables them to have more than one defining characteristic.

But every time you try to innovate a material in architecture, you are taking a huge risk. By working with a manufacturer who will produce that material, we share the responsibilities and are able to test the viability of a material's performance or maintenance over time.

12

Scogin You can't experiment. You have to be absolutely sure that a product is going to work, unless a client is willing to invest in an experiment that may or may not work. And so there are tremendous limitations on what you can do. In terms of the exterior of a building, it's extremely difficult to take risks.

We had that house up in Maine. It's got these silly panels on it; it's got 35,000 stainless steel screws, and I don't know how many miles of joints that are just caulked. Well, you know—30 degrees below zero in the winter and 85 degrees in the summer—one could say that that was really a risk. But since we had a carpenter who was willing to try it, and we had a builder who did it perfectly, it has never been a problem. But it's probably something I'd never try again, because it is just too risky. (laughter) A lot of people call and ask about those kinds of things, and I've tried to discourage them, frankly, because it's risky. I don't know if that is the kind of risk you are talking about. But I can't tell you how embarrassing it is when you try a material detail and it doesn't work—it's really bad. (laughter)

Kennedy I want to take a slightly more optimistic note. I think that some issues about building are really market-driven, and the fact that the bottom dropped out of the NASDAQ recently is only going to underscore the need to reassess what a building skin can be and what its long-term life cycle will cost. It's my opinion that we will be driven by market forces to reevaluate a lot of architectural building materials and standards. In fact, one of our clients, New York City's EDC, is now requiring that we use photovoltaic and solid-state lighting in the design of the East River Ferry Terminals because it just makes sense. Solid-state technologies that can operate continuously for more than ten years are more durable than many conventional building products. So there's a demand for this out there, and in a short period of time, that demand will be translated to the institutional and private sectors.

I was recently in Washington, D.C., at a congressional hearing on opto-electronics technology. The government is going to sponsor a major research initiative through challenge grants that will be distributed to leading universities.

Despite the risks in creating and using new materials, the intellectual rewards are greater; there are many interesting opportunities. I feel that architectural education— the architectural imagination that we all share—is going to be a valuable resource to bring to bear in this emerging situation that is already affecting us all.

Nader Tehrani How are they funding this research? Is it through scientific labs? Or is it making it into the architectural schools? Because another tendency, when the NASDAQ falls, is to retract and concentrate on risk management, which is the opposite of what you are describing. So how is this being done? Is it through grants?

Kennedy Some is done through grants, some through direct commissions. So it can be financed through a variety of mechanisms. In the case of the government, the Department of Energy will distribute the research funds. It may seem counterintuitive, but a focus that only minimizes risk doesn't offer the government or manufacturers the best position for success.

13

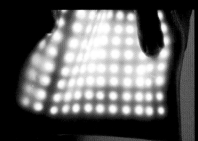

Light Information Desk
Kennedy & Violich Architecture
2001

The Light Information Desk com-
bines the material properties of
acrylic polymer, the mobile characteristics of furniture, and the trans-
missive properties of lighting and
communications infrastructure. The
intelligent organization of light inter-
sects with the potential to take com-
putation into the built environment,
allowing information exchange to
become a function of architectural
surfaces. A personalized digital pro-
file may extend from the computer
screen into the proximate environment of the workplace. Served by
fiber-optic relays and a series of
solid-state components, the transparent acrylic surface functions as a
light guide to transport light (color)
and information through the desk in
response to a diverse series of work
tasks. The luminosity of the Light
Information Desk creates an energy
efficient ambient lighting that sup-
ports reduced external light loads.
This results in a more strategic use
of illumination over an entire office
building, producing long- and short-
term savings and significant reduction of environmental impacts.

Give Back Curtain
Kennedy & Violich Architecture
2000-ongoing

The Give Back Curtain is part of a
series of techno-fabric designs that
extend the modern architectural tradition of the portable screen. The
Give Back Curtain brings to a pliable
fabric matrix the capacity to conduct
and deliver light through a fabrication process that integrates photolu-
minescent pigments in synthetic or
natural fibers. Sunlight or fluorescent light is absorbed by the fabric
and then given back as visible colored light. Unlike traditional woven
fabrics, the Give Back Curtain is a
dynamic medium. The cloth produces
a pattern of specific temporal characteristics that changes color and
figuration over time. A lacework of
semiconductors can be woven into
the fabric to control light input and
extend light delivery. Applications
include increasing light intensity by
bundling and folding fabric surfaces,
and transporting light physically
through luminous privacy enclosures
in residential, commercial, and
workplace settings.

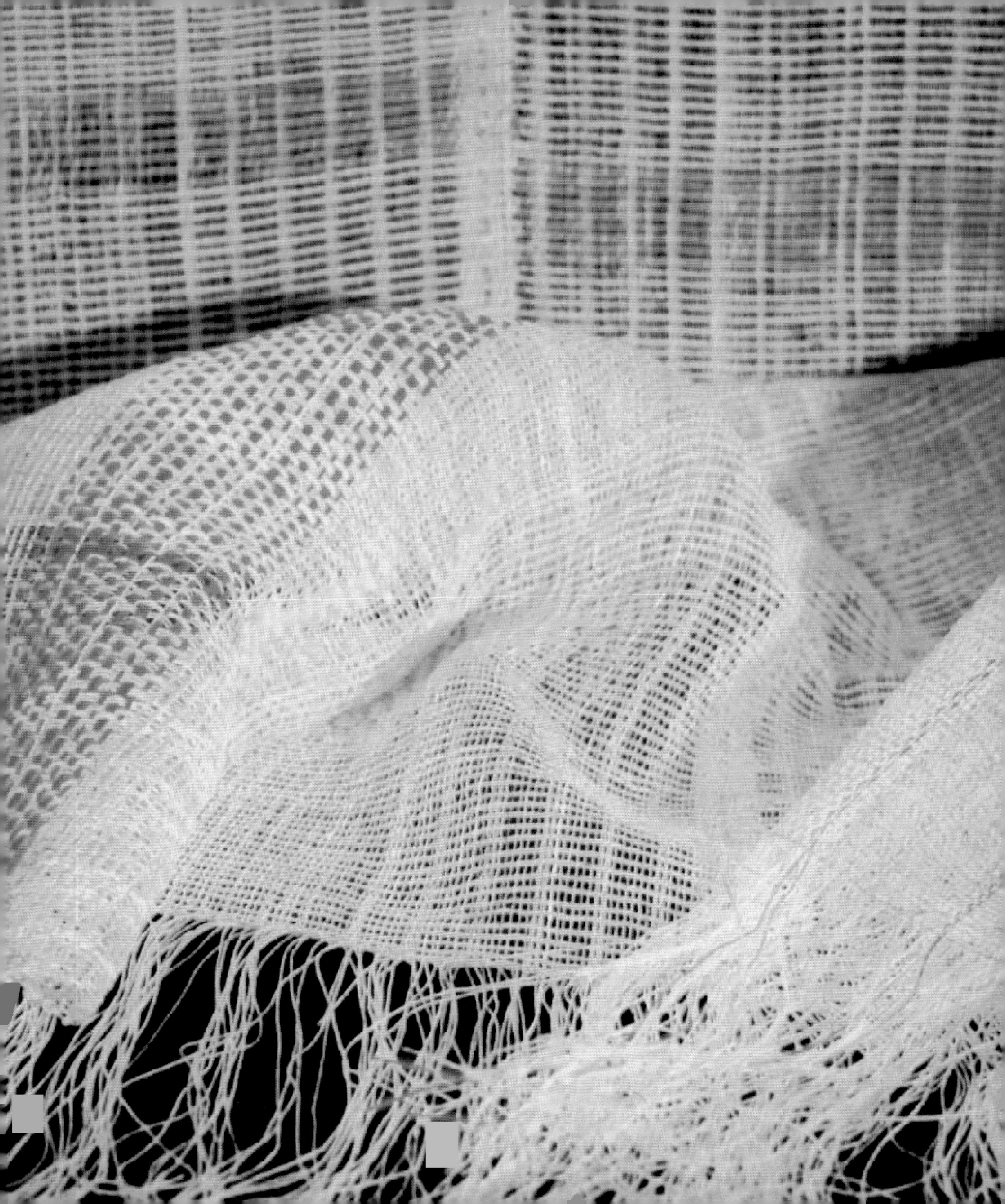

Mori After World War II, there was this whole movement in the 1950s, exemplified by Case Study houses in California, modernist houses in New Canaan, and new houses in Sarasota, Florida. They were all experimental, and the architects were highly creative with materials. And if you look closely at those houses, they were inexpensive and roughly put together: some leaked, some did not last long, and they were actually more like prototypes. It seems to me that the four of you do that type of visionary work. But even though you put forward these experiments, you are also very responsible in terms of the performance of the buildings: you detail everything to last. We learned some lessons from those earlier generations, so that the experimentation you do is slightly different—more calculated.

Hawkinson Rudolph Schindler's Kings Road House is a really early example, and it's very rough. I love that house, but at the same time it is incredibly funky. A lot of experiments were done in this house not just to use material for material's sake, but were related to the way one lived: you could sleep outdoors, natural light could come in, or you

Smith-Miller + Hawkinson Architects, Pier 11, Wall Street Ferry Pier

could have a fireplace that was both inside and out. Or the kitchen might be for two people. So the experiments had a kind of agenda related to use.

Kennedy The thing that is interesting is that by redefining program, Schindler redefines the role of the architect. It's not clear in my mind that the role of the architect is only to design buildings—I probably don't want to say that here! (laughter) Could we imagine a broader palette of activities? Could we imagine architects creating new programs and applications for materials? Could we imagine architects being involved in different global platforms that influence cultural production? It could be very liberating. The first job I had after I graduated from school was to design lines of lighting. Architects are able to enter into any one of the other sets of related design disciplines and make a contribution.

Hawkinson I think there's a certain power that, potentially, the architect can garner if one makes associations to the process of fabrication and to the people who are actually making the material. You're no longer subject to the middle person who has an incredible

Smith-Miller + Hawkinson Architects, Pier 11, Wall Street Ferry Pier

amount of power and control— the construction manager. Right? (laughter) It allows the architect to go around this person and establish relationships with manufacturers, while also advancing the process of rapid prototyping, or expediting the shop drawing. I'm very optimistic about this type of arrangement, and I find it incredibly exciting. When I walked around today to see what you guys are doing here in the basement—I really think that's the future of our profession.

Mori Mack, do you think that professional practice is going to change soon? Or is our society conservative and resistant in terms of letting architects supervise the other trades?

Scogin No, I would second what Laurie just said. I think there is a definitive future for the profession of architecture right now in this realm of empowerment—of more authority, more input. Architects are now able to envision and realize a structure that was not realizable just a few years ago. And they are beginning to understand that to make those things, they've got to work closely with the people who literally put things together. And they have also realized that the only way to do that is to bypass or reinvent the process that's out there now.

17

Smith-Miller + Hawkinson Architects, Canopy, La Guardia Airport

18

Frank Gehry's the classic example, at this point, of how to make that happen. He has invented a new type of practice out of a desire to realize his design work. It involves technology and an entire restructuring of the practice of architecture—legally, contractually—and a redefinition of the relationship between owner, architect, and contractor. What's exciting about it is that you realize that you can do some new type of architecture, but to make it happen, you've got to reinvent the profession. It is such a great example because you realize that the product—or the building, or the piece of architecture—is what drives it all. It pays off; it's exciting to the public. It is work that inspires change: cultural change, economic change, and political change. It has invigorated the whole discussion around the evolution of practice. So I agree with both Laurie and Sheila: it is a great future for architects. But it's not just about materials; it's also about design and structure—it's the whole creative process that is actually driving it.

What Sheila's work suggests is that you can go about this in a number of different ways. The thing that sets us apart as architects is this structured, creative thinking that other people don't bring to it—that's our ace. That's what empowers us for the future.

Marco Steinberg Let me play devil's advocate. I question whether Gehry is the right model, given the resources he's working with. He's actually quite privileged: the subcontractors he's working with are willing to take on liability. These issues of risk, innovation, and direct influence in the process are ultimately liability issues. But is it generally feasible for a sole-proprietor architect to have sufficient leverage to take on such liabilities?

Scogin I don't think it has anything to do with scale. I've seen people like Nader and Sheila making things and entering into the profession in ways that that haven't been done before. You have to invent the processes; you have to invent the contracts. And you have to find ways to take on the liability. When I was in architecture school, you were taught to do it this way; this is the way to do it. These are the invariable other ways, but why would you bother with other ways? Now, I think the attitude in young practitioners I see is that they're figuring out ways to accomplish these things. They don't have to operate like Frank Gehry—they find their own way.

Tehrani   I wanted to get back to Marco's question. I'm not sure how Sheila and Frano are doing it, but in our case, we are losing a tremendous amount of money. And we're exposing ourselves in ways that ultimately and probably—

Audience   Just like Schindler. (laughter)

Tehrani   And I only want to become rich. (laughter) So I'm wondering, are there ways to get institutional support, whether through the AIA or other kinds of institutionalized frameworks to change practice?

Mori   The last time Gehry was here, I had a conversation with him about transforming practice. He said that we should mobilize and insure ourselves. He actually does believe it; he wants to institute that. And I think that's fabulous. If we don't get together and do something about it, insurance companies and lawyers are going to take over our profession. "Why should we give them extra money?" is his attitude, I think, and he is absolutely right.

Ron Witte   I want to go back to Sheila's earlier observation. The issue of the crisis, I think, is one that has more or less gone away. And that's because technology operates to synthesize. A very simple example: AutoCAD lets me draw something, and it lets me send that file to a fabricator. It also lets me attach a certain amount of quantitative information to that thing, which could include economy. And I could, with the push of a button, more or less—I could send all of that information to two or three points. And all of that information gets processed—one hopes —simultaneously. So before the economist can tell me that this is a bad idea, the fabricator has told me it can be done. There's nothing magic about AutoCAD, but there are things like that which enable the Gehry model or other models to flow through, in all kinds of iterations. So for me the crisis is gone, and that's what leads to optimism.

Kennedy   No, for me the crisis is not gone. (laughter) But maybe the word "crisis" is too theatrical. I really mean a predicament of value when we think about materials. And if you think about material strategies in architecture that persist today, there is room for expansion! There's a kind of postmodernist elevation of low materials, as exemplified in the research of Scott Brown and Venturi. Then there's another approach, seen in Peter Zumthor's thermal baths, where materials are used to evoke the authenticity of an experience. But although the materials are natural stone, it is highly artificial how they're put together. So it's a really interesting moment right now in the culture of material history. I enjoy being in it because I think that we can shift and push those values. I don't think they're static. The whole set of terms that we inherited from modernism is thus completely up for grabs: natural, artificial, culture, technology, materiality, media. These terms are coming together, and it makes them very interesting and unstable. That's what I mean by "crisis of materiality." So where I agree with Ron is that each person, as an architect, probably needs to deal with that shifting terrain and articulate a path for themselves, in their work and in their own position vis-à-vis materials. Because we can't take materials and their cultural properties for granted.

19

surface

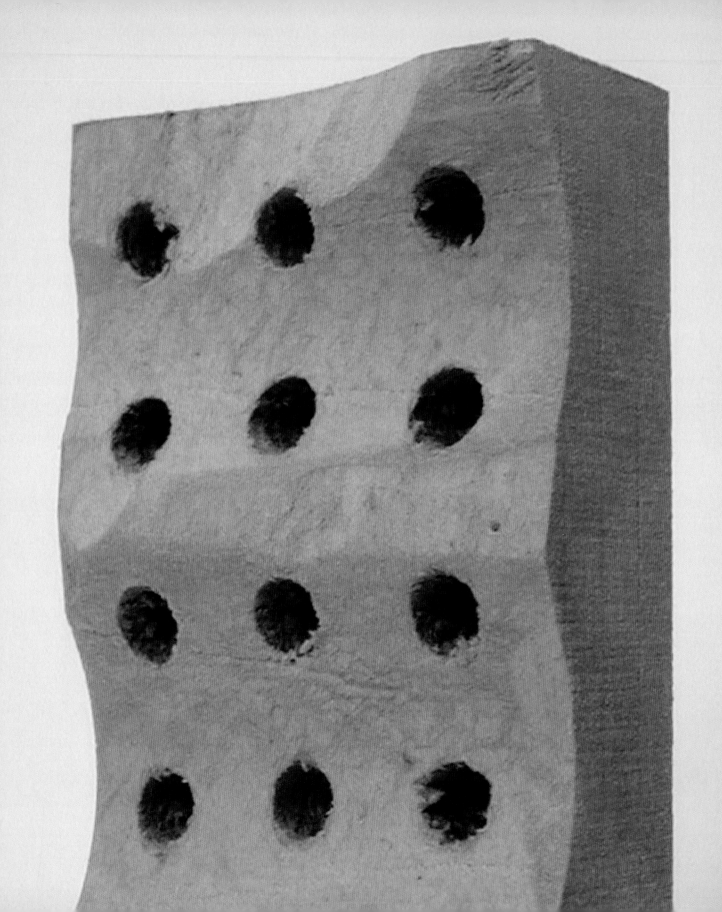

surface

MARCO STEINBERG

Construction-related materials often have latent possibilities that extend well beyond the uses for which they were created. Usually generated in response to quantitative criteria, these materials tend to have significant (though often unsuspected) potential for innovation and progress. Our research objective was to find opportunities for innovation while testing our role—and limitations—as designers in material processes.

In the recent history of materials, there has been a great increase in the number and variety of engineered products. As a result of selective performance engineering, homogeneous, task-oriented materials have proliferated. Good at specific, quantitative applications, they seem to lack the complexity and character of traditional materials. How then might one design with a material devoid of the "warmth" and "grain" of wood? We decided to regard these very qualities of anonymity and homogeneity as positive attributes. Character in these engineered materials has to be established—and exploited—on very different terms. Our research sought to lay the groundwork for new applications beyond the original mandate of the material.

Recently innovation has been associated with advances in technology, a model that architecture and the building industry have been quick to appropriate. Tying innovation exclusively to new technology, however, can prove reductive. Our work attempts to frame innovation within a larger definition of design. Innovation in this work comes through the application of imagination, by asking a basic question: What have we not yet perceived in the commonplace materials surrounding us?

The research set out to explore this moment of intersection between design, materials, and production. The specific interest was in industrially based construction materials understood both as products and as processes. Ultimately the research was productive in its pedagogy, its direct products, and in the questions it raised. The work also explored opportunities for the development of a praxis of research—something that is sorely missing in design. Currently "design research" typically borrows from either historical/theoretical or scientific models and has yet to establish a clear methodology of its own.

After surveying common construction-based panel products, we identified three that fulfilled certain requirements. All materials had to be industrially manufactured, task oriented, and commonly available, and have engineered properties (quantitative criteria). We identified gypsum board, recycled paper–based fiberboard (see box), and medium-density fiberboard as promising candidates. Next we targeted three levels of design impact: (1) within the property of the material, (2) within the manufacturing process, and (3) within the perceived value of the product.

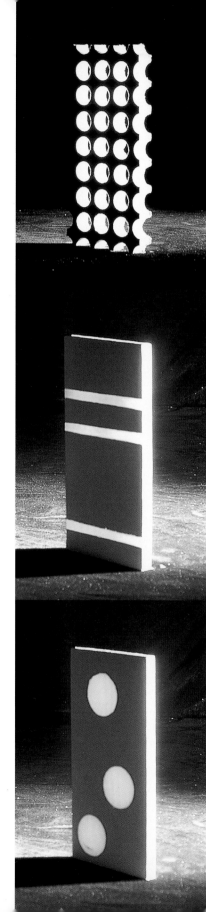

Working directly within material properties seemed the most difficult and would assume a level of sophistication about the science of materials not necessarily appropriate for a designer. This left two primary areas that were explored in the research: process and perception. Perception would prove to be the most fertile ground for exploration, and here the notion of design as an act of both imagination and transformation was fundamental.

Following the terms set in an initial research brief, we sought to transform the material at hand into panel samples. These reconstituted samples should be continuous (or suggest how they might be). We focused on verbs as a way of thinking about materials in terms of their processes: cut, cast, mold, extrude, etc. Having acted on the material, we produced an effect, or quality. We sought to uncover and begin to catalog these qualities.

We kept the samples to a single term. For example, by slicing (action) we can produce a very thin (quality) product. We developed a taxonomy for these "qualitative" samples, making a chart that described the actions to be undertaken and then setting them up against possible variables (for example, if the term is "grind," then the rows for that column might exploit a range of options such as course, fine, etc.). We established the upper and lower limits of the category and described how properties are altered, looking for critical dimensional or procedural thresholds. At the end of each iteration, we posted our best sample boards, which were made dimensionally equal to foster discussion through comparison.

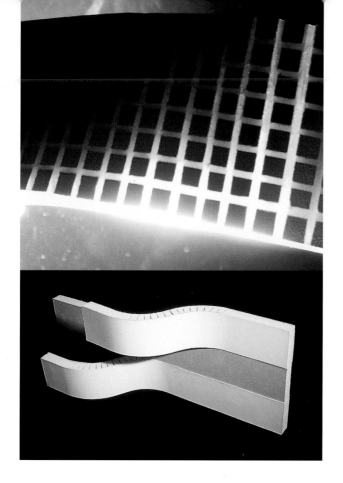

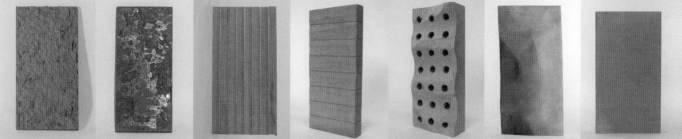

and product easily lend themselves to the imagination of architects. With this work, we hope to reimagine simple industrial materials in significant and unprecedented ways.

pers, correspondence, and the odd aluminum gum wrapper are received by the manufacturing plant, screened for any impurities (non-paper-based products or cardboards), and sent to a large pulping machine. The machine adds water and blends printing ink and paper into a soft gray slurry. As if in a giant blender the pulp swirls around, loosening fibers for future rearrangement. Through a network of pipes the slurry is sent to a form, where water is extracted from the slurry and the sheet pressed. On this thick sheet of fine papier-mâché, starch binds the fibers. Water extracted through the fine metal mesh of the formwork leaves a finely dimpled

rigidity and stability. As the sheets emerge, a fine, irregular yellowing of the edges becomes visible— the expression of the impact of water extraction and heat on the greater surface-area-to-volume ratio of the edge. The now rigid sheet is sent to postproduction, where cutting and sanding impart distinctly different qualities: sanding gives it a velvety, fabric-like surface, while the serrated edge of the bandsaw results in a fine, toothlike grain. Defective sheets are sent back to the blender and transformed once again into slurry.

This sample-based process of the early research phase was initially based on trial and error. After we gained a clear sense of the range of material expression, more specific applications were generated. These applications would ultimately prove decisive, as they tested the way in which ideas could find expression. Recycled paper–based fiberboard—because of its easy workability—was merely a means to an end, not an end in itself.

Left largely in the hands of science, material development in the construction industry has been primarily driven by quantitative criteria. Based on volume rather than margin, its serial manufacturability ultimately guarantees homogeneity. Within the serial manufacturing of a material, however, exists the possibility for design. Hardly the result of empirical science alone, material production is driven as much—if not more—by the values of a culture. As such it is imperative that designers reclaim a voice in the molding of these values.

Note

Bill Yen, Kristine Synnes, Dan Cheong, Jeremy Ficca, and Stephanie Grandjacques contributed to the research described here.

ROUNDTABLE DISCUSSION *with shigeru ban*

Shigeru Ban's ingenuity as an architect arises from several characteristics that reflect his personal beliefs and worldview. First, his economy of means is shown in his minimalist design aesthetic, which translates literally to his sparing use of materials. In addition, his frugality is based on an extremely pragmatic approach to finding the least expensive and most accessible means to an end. This tendency is also reflected in his ecological attitude of carefully avoiding waste and encouraging reuse and recycling of materials. His sometimes humorous scavenger mentality leads him to cleverly appropriate materials fabricated for other purposes for new uses. He has also learned from the traditional Japanese wisdom of making do with weak materials such as wood and paper. In short, he is an idealistic pragmatist with a humanitarian mission at the core of his activities.

Toshiko Mori Shigeru Ban is noted for his use of paper as a building material; he has pushed the limits of the materiality of paper in architecture. The question is which came first, the program or the material? For example, for an emergency shelter—did the program come first? Or did it come about while you were pursuing the materiality of paper? And how did it become a real project?

Shigeru Ban I'm sure that the material came first. Since I started developing the paper tube structure in 1986, I knew that this material was very strong—much stronger than I expected—and we can produce it almost anywhere in the world. And now I am preparing shelters in India, after the earthquake. We have already found a good paper tube manufacturer near the disaster area; many small manufacturers provide tubes to use in the textile factories. So we found a local manufacturer near

Left: Shigeru Ban Architects, Nemunoki Art Museum, 1999
Above: Shigeru Ban Architects, Japan Pavilion, Hannover Expo 2000

Above: Shigeru Ban Architects, Paper House, 1995

Facing page: Shigeru Ban Architects, Imai Hospital Day Care Center, 2001

the disaster site in Ahmedabad. I'm also using plastic beer containers as a foundation, but I could not find a plastic beer container at the site because nobody drinks beer there. So my local partner proposed that we use Coca-Cola containers. However, I didn't want to use something that didn't have a local character.

Mori   Of course you don't want to promote monopoly and global consumerism; you would rather promote local business.

Ban   Yes, but I may not have a choice, if they give us everything for free. I'd like to find some local company that would volunteer to donate. That was one of the interesting characteristics of the paper tube project. After a disaster, the price of building material always goes up because of the scarcity. But since paper tubes are not a typical building material, they are very easy to get, even after a disaster. And it is inexpensive: I got all the material for free when I built temporary houses in Turkey in 1999. So that's why I thought this material would be really appropriate for temporary shelters.

I proposed this idea to the United Nations High Commission for Refugees (UNHCR) in 1994 when they were dealing with the crisis in Rwanda. They had some problems with finding an alternative material to replace wood. In general the United Nations provided refugees with plastic sheeting only, and they had to cut trees to make a frame for the plastic. In Rwanda, more than 2 million people became refugees, and they were cutting trees all over the place, leading to serious deforestation and environmental problems. Previously the UN had provided them with aluminum pipes, so that they would stop cutting trees. But aluminum was an expensive material, and so the refugees sold the pipes for money and started cutting trees again. That's why the UNHCR accepted my proposal to use the paper tube as an alternative material. So, anyway, the material came first. I thought, "This is really appropriate for a temporary shelter," and then I came up with the proposal. That is how I started.

Mori Did you develop the paper tubes themselves in any way? Did you come up with a system of fabrication to make it structural? Or did you work with manufacturers or structural engineers to develop it and specifically make it into a shelter?

Ban Actually, I have not done anything special; I'm just using existing material for other purposes. It is almost impossible for a single person to invent something really new, so the only thing that we can do as individuals is to use existing material to serve different purposes. The paper tube is one of them. It is usually used for storing textiles, and in the field of architecture it is used as formwork to make round concrete posts. The industry has already developed many ways of waterproofing the paper tube itself, using film, polyurethane, and polyacrylic paint. I'm just using the existing technology. I didn't develop anything new or even add anything to make this material strong. I have no interest in making a material stronger—I'm just using it the way it is.

For example, I designed the Paper Dome in 1998. Each time I design a different type of structure in paper, I have to get the government's per-

Shigeru Ban Architects, Nemunoki Art Museum, 1999

mission to use the paper tube as a structural element by showing data on the engineering calculations. I used the straight joists connected by laminated timber joints to make the arch. I knew that timber joints are relatively expensive, but they became inexpensive with the paper tubes. Also, one of the interesting characteristics of the paper tube is that we can make anything out of it. To make it even more economical, this time I didn't want to use a wooden joint, because that's quite expensive. Here in Germany, for the Japanese Pavilion at Hannover

Expo 2000, we knew we could transport the paper tube in lengths of up to 20 meters (67 feet) on the highway. We used very long tubes—about 20 meters—and we connected them to make an even longer tube, and so this is the first time that I've used a longer joist. The diameter is about 12 centimeters (4 3/4 inches) and the thickness is less than one inch. It's waterproofed by polyurethane both inside and out. And we tested it for extreme weather and fire protection. This material is very difficult to burn because of the density of the paper. We simply connected it with fabric tape at every intersection.

We didn't want to use heavy machines to erect the structure, so we designed it to be erected by hand. One of the main themes of the Expo was environmental issues. My idea was to use recycled paper —recycled in Germany—and after they demolished the building, all the material would once again be recycled. We used only one piece of high-tech equipment, a GPS satellite system: we would measure the change of the shape every day from a satellite, so that we could correct the shape. We also developed a waterproof, fireproof paper membrane; usually we use a PVC membrane, but PVC would make dioxin, which is wasted; therefore we didn't want to use a PVC membrane for a temporary structure. That's why all the lighting comes through the paper, and at night it becomes like a lantern designed by Isamu Noguchi. Instead of using mechanical joints, we just used fabric tape, which allows the paper tube to move in a complicated way. Also it is naturally post-tensioned.

Mori Is the tube also arching as a result of the vaulting?

Ban Yes, it's bending a little.

Mori Is there a limit to how much it can bend?

Ban We tested how much we can bend it because, if we bend the tubes too much, then the stress remains in the tubes and weakens them.

Mori Was your tape tied down manually?

Ban Yes; it's very simple—it's just like a buckle. We just put the fabric tape to the buckle and pull. But it doesn't have to be really tight, because it moves along this knot— it pushes and gives tension automatically, so that it doesn't have to be knotted to be strong. Our paper membrane is also rather weak, so the maximum size we could make the sides was 3 meters by 3 meters. We added a wooden frame for the paper membrane, which triangulates the paper grid shell. We also used a ladder for the construction, completion, and maintenance. But originally the dimensions of this section of wood were much smaller. In Germany the authorities didn't want to accept anything new, so they tried to make my structure as conventional as possible, and they made the dimension of the section four times bigger than necessary. Therefore this is not a pure paper tube structure but a hybrid structure between paper and wood, because of that compromise. But to get permission, I had to compromise.

I didn't want to use a concrete foundation, because concrete is difficult to recycle. So I made a wooden box filled with sand to support the structure. Another interesting material is paper honeycomb, which we used in the joints. I had previously designed another project in Japan using this paper honeycomb as a part of a structure. In our Nemunoki Art Museum for Disabled Children, we agreed with the client not to use artificial light; we wanted to get light from the ceiling. We then used this experience to make the testing procedure shorter for the Hannover Pavilion. The most difficult thing in using paper is getting permission from the government; it's very complicated. The structure for the Museum of Modern Art, the Paper Arch, is purely a paper tube structure. The sides of the structure are much smaller than Hannover because we didn't have to work with mean German authorities.

Mori Does a structural engineer figure out actual stresses? Or is it more low-tech?

Ban I use one of the top engineers to analyze everything. For Hannover, I worked with Professor Frei Otto and the engineering firm in England, Buro Huppold, to design the structure. Huppold also had an office in New York, so we could use all the testing data from Hannover for the MoMA project.

Mori Did you work with the late Gengo Matsumoto, a legendary Japanese structural engineer, to develop the paper tube?

Ban Yes, in the beginning I worked with Professor Matsumoto to start this structure. Then, after he passed away, I started working with another engineer and Professor Otto to develop this further. I always depend on really good engineers.

Marco Steinberg How does the material affect your use of structure, and your attitude toward the structural technique? It seems that you are essentially using the paper tubes to simulate timber?

Ban No, I don't think so, because the paper tube is weaker than wood, and it is softer. Wood cannot bend this much in this size. That is one important way for me to take advantage of the paper tube itself. Also, this cannot be designed with bamboo either, although it looks somewhat like bamboo. I didn't have any interest in using bamboo for the structure, because traditionally there are already so many wonderful structural designs with bamboo. Even Renzo Piano tried to design a bamboo structure, and he didn't succeed. Many engineers have tried to use bamboo for modern construction. But bamboo is a weak material because its diameter is widely varied, and its thickness also varies. That is why it is difficult to test the structure, which makes it hard to apply bamboo to modern design.

Paper tubes are almost a high-tech material. It's an industrial material over which we can control the quality and the strength. And that's why we can calculate it. I've told you that I didn't invent anything new; I'm just using the existing material in a different way. It is very important to throw away preconceptions.

When I designed a train station, I wanted to use precast concrete piles as the columns and little timber beams, but I was told by the authority—the Japan Metal Company—that I couldn't use wooden construction for the

Shinkansen train station. So here I arranged the steel like sandwiches —very thin—to take care of the load for the bending. The wooden beam I used is a small fragment. It is not a continuous beam, because it is wood and not supporting any bending movement. It's just protecting the stress and stiffening the steel plate for deflection. So this works as a kind of hybrid structure between wood and steel.

Afterward, I thought about how this wood could offer fire protection to the steel itself. Have you heard of "oversizing" in wood construction? When you want to design a fire-protective wood structure, this method is already approved in many countries. The oversizing means that we have to design the corners and beams of the timber to be bigger than necessary. For example, if we oversize one inch bigger than the structure's necessary size, the oversizing works as a protection of the wood for a half hour.

So my idea is to use the wooden panel around the steel columns, or beams, because the wood doesn't transfer heat. If our wood is burned, it will become charcoal. And charcoal works as good fire protection. I tested this in the field, and the result was much better

than I expected: it works as fire protection and also as a final finish. Usually you have to spray ugly fire protection on the steel, which then has to be covered. And then you have to apply a final finish to the wood or steel. So this idea was used for the construction of the GC Building.

Mori Are stress-bearing diagrams similar for the paper tubes as they are for wood?

Ban Yes, the tubes are very similar to wood. It's almost an engineered wood, because of the layer of the paper. And the paper still has the fiber. But after the paper is recycled again and again, the fiber gets shorter and becomes weaker.

Mori Perhaps you can talk about your recent work using innovative methods to construct emergency shelters. You built temporary houses from paper tubes after the Kobe earthquake in 1995, and then in Turkey.

Ban We had to improve the insulation in Turkey because the winter is very cold, and they have snow. Children helped us to put waste paper inside the tubes to make them more insulated. It's as simple that: if you put anything inside, it acts as insulation. We already tested this insulation, and it works

34

well. Although I didn't want to spend too much money for each shelter, I recommended that the residents put some corrugated cardboard on the walls to make it more insulated.

Mori What about durability of materials?

Ban In traditional Japanese architecture, we invented beautiful joinery. Yet wood is a weak material that is vulnerable to both water and termites. When a part of wood begins to fail, we just cut it to replace the damaged structure, using some of the joinery. In Japan there are many traditional buildings—some more than 500, 600 years old. And the life span of the building has nothing to do with the durability of the material. Concrete buildings are easily destroyed by earthquake, and masonry structures—concrete, brick—are difficult to repair. But structures like wood, or even paper tubes, are so lightweight that are resistant to earthquake damage and easy to repair or replace if damaged. That's why I don't care about the durability of the paper—because if there is some damage, we can easily repair or replace the material. That's why I think it's going to be a permanent material.

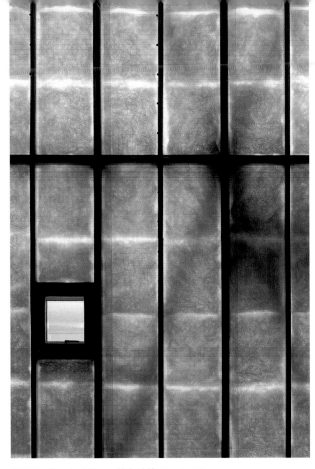

Shigeru Ban Architects, Naked House, 2000

Mori Because it can be easily repaired and maintained. Therefore one can assume that it can last forever—as long as one is willing to maintain it.

Ban Yes, for example, concrete is more dangerous because you cannot maintain it by yourself, and you cannot see how much the concrete is damaged inside. It just suddenly collapses. But with a paper tube structure, the failure or problem will be visible.

Mori Please talk about your recent house project.

Ban In this project, the site is in an agricultural area. I tried to use the context the way it was. So for the older, outside skin, I used corrugated fiberglass panels with a double layer horizontally and vertically to strengthen it—it's like plywood. The space in-between also works as insulation. The client's request was very interesting: he said he wanted to have a house like a warehouse. He didn't need the strict privacy of individual rooms; he wanted to share time and space with his family. So I designed it like a warehouse—just one big space, but with four movable individual rooms. You can change the position of the rooms wherever you want, even if it's going outside, to sleep outside.

Inside the house has a fabric skin. This fabric is normally used outside for canopies, so it is very durable. It is also easy to take it out to wash it or to change the fabric, and it is translucent. Between this fabric and the fiberglass, there are two layers of insulation. One is the noodle-shaped foam-core material that is usually used for packing fruit. We put it in clear plastic bags. It works as insulation, but it is also translucent, and the next layer is bubble-wrap. I put bubble-wrap in between the fabric and the noodle type of insulation to make another layer. Then inside is this fabric screen to make the wall translucent. Two sides of individual rooms are sliding doors; if you take away the sliding doors, you can connect the four rooms. The layout of the rooms is very flexible.

Mori One of the interesting things is that you are using existing materials.

Ban Exactly.

Mori Usually nonstructural materials—and more humble ones: paper tubes, and packing materials. And plywood. And at the same time, I assume that many of these materials are universally available?

Ban Yes.

Mori But you are actually making a new language of architecture. There is tremendous irony when you say, "I made paper architecture." (laughter)

Ban Yes, because there is a history at Cooper Union of using "paper architecture" as a theoretical model. And I have to carry on that legacy.

Mori So you have to carry on (laughter), with this incredible sense of irony and wisdom. You are suddenly changing the language of architecture; we know wood and steel and concrete as pillars, as conventional architectural materials, and now something as strange as paper tubes are introduced, which are common and overlap with consumer products.

Ban Right.

Mori How do you think of that unusual shift in material use from convention?

Ban Well, I am lucky—my clients are always very poor. (laughter) The budget is always very limited. I have to use humble, cheap materials and make them into a real project. But it is still a good way of training myself.

Nader Tehrani I'm interested in the costs of the kinds of experimentations you do and how that gets accommodated in the budgets. First of all, just the cost of having to get things approved by a regulatory agency, and second, the time factor.

Ban I'm terrible about calculations, except for the client's budget; I'm very strict about keeping costs down. But I never calculate the man-hours, the man-days, that are required for our research.

Tehrani Do you count on, for example, manufacturers who are willing to contribute to the experimentation because they are going to sell the products?

Ban Well, generally manufacturers don't see any advantage in supporting us because we are not using a particular product. That's why I always have to invest my money and time to do it. If I calculate my man-days, it isn't worth it at all.

Tehrani Are you always finding better mechanisms for getting this testing done? Are you finding new ways to deal with new codes, or do you see this effort as contributing to the restructuring of regulations in Japan?

Ban Well, yes—that's an interesting point. Because each time I design a different type of structure in paper, I have to get different permission. It takes time and money. I may get a big project in Japan to build a paper structure. And I went to the construction authorities to discuss it. And now, after three years, they have become more flexible. They tried to allow some kind of exception to the law, to accept the paper tube as a building material, because of my previous experience. But it is strange that they would make such an exception for paper tubes, because nobody else is using them. This exception would work only for me. (laughter)

Steinberg Historically, some designers have sought to direct the attention of the observer to structural innovations, while others tried to mask the innovation. Where do you position yourself within a lineage of structural expressionism as a deliberate act?

Ban One thing that might be different from the traditional wood approach is that usually you invent different material for a new structure to make the structure act more acrobatically, or to try to make it thinner or produce a so-called high-tech expression. But my interest is not in making stronger material; I always try to use the weak material the way it is. Because of the weak material, I have to use a bigger size, and repeat elements many times. That characterizes the space and the architecture. When you invent new materials and structure, you can get new kinds of space. Instead of just using the design or the style, I want to develop the material—and the structure—to design a different kind of space, using the special character of the material.

Mori You employ this strategy in humanitarian venues. What is this organization you started?

Ban I work for the UN as a consultant, but also I have my own organization—VAN (Voluntary Architects Network)—to do projects in disaster areas. But I have to raise money by myself to do it.

Mori Well, that's an amazing activity: you have volunteers, and you do fundraising. You're very proactive as an architect.

Ban So as long as I can build something, it's satisfying my desire. And to me, building an expensive house and making a refugee shelter is the same thing. As long as I can make something somewhere, I satisfy myself. And also, the appreciation of the client…. They are all the same, after they move in. The way they show me their satisfaction—it's really the same.

37

substance

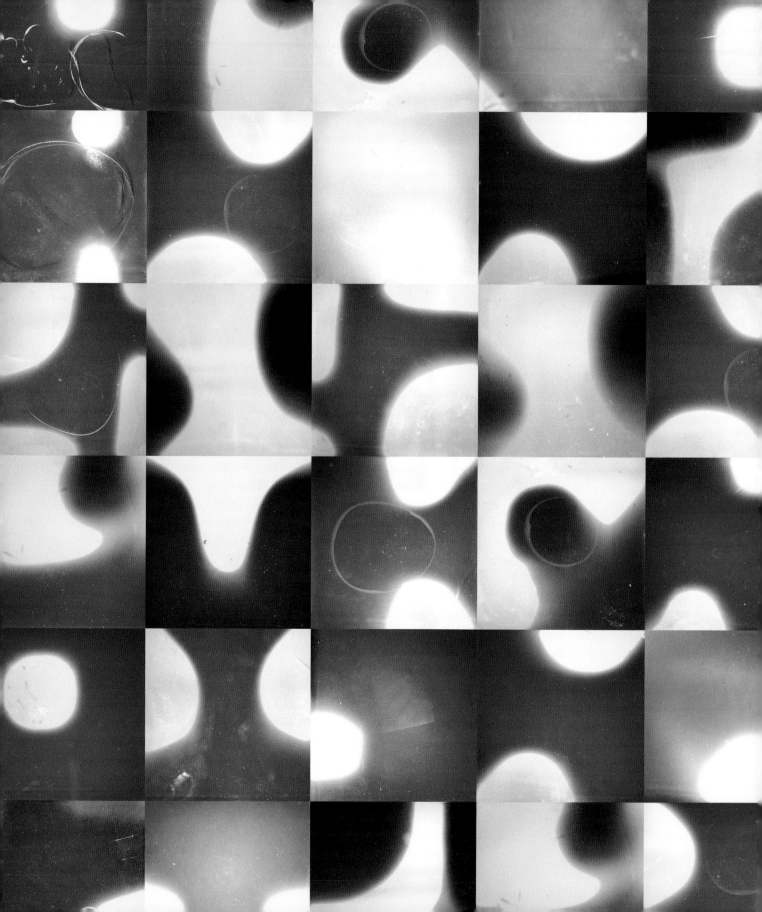

substance

RON WITTE

with Billie Faircloth, Judith Hodge, Suzanne Kim, and Clover Lee

Ninety-eight Percent Nothing

There is a curious thickness about architecture's thinness today. Even as they have grown ever thinner, building skins have developed an appetite for more: more performance, more sensuousness, more intelligence, more more. The virtues of the thin have been fattened by the capacity of contemporary materials to absorb, affect, and assimilate. Refusing a singular loyalty to function, technology, or form, these materials are unabashed in their collective acceleration of commodity, firmness, and delight. Technically exacting in their pursuit of performance, such materials also provoke reassessments of some of architecture's principal aesthetic subjectivities: proportion, form, and perhaps even beauty itself.

Aerogel, a silica-based substance that is 98 percent nothing—air—is one such material. A one-inch cube of aerogel contains a total surface area equal to that of a basketball court. Its fabrication begins with the suspension of a low-density silica chemistry in a liquid solvent. This solvent is then extracted in an autoclave, leaving an ultrafine glass matrix of hollow cavities. The combination of aerogel's adaptable characteristics—an aerogel surface can migrate freely across transparent, translucent, and opaque physiognomies—and its liquid origins provoked us to reconsider the conceptual frameworks used by architects to organize material systems. We focused on the fact that these materials are detailed at the scale of microns rather than feet and inches and,

as a result, they produce surfaces comprised of material contours rather than assemblies of parts. To better evaluate characteristics of material contouring at a larger scale, we conducted a parallel research project that led to the fabrication of a series of large-scale cast resin panels. This supplemental work allowed us to refine the geometries of the mold/material relationship at a size that is currently not tenable with aerogel due to the dimensional constraints of the autoclave that we used.

The Ninety-eight Percent Nothing project investigated surfaces comprised of differentiated optical or structural zones whose material composition remained, nonetheless, entirely homogeneous. Throughout this work, our primary interest was in an exploration of differentiable homogeneity—what we termed "variant-sameness"—in materials.

Redefining the persistent binary of "window" and "wall" that permeates architecture was central to our variant-sameness research. Aerogel's extraordinary insulation value—a single-inch thickness of the material insulates as effectively as thirty-two layers of glass—obviates any need to distinguish between walls and windows for thermal reasons. Introducing carbon into the normally transparent aerogel chemistry creates an opacity spectrum ranging from entirely clear to entirely opaque that similarly collapses the distinction between window

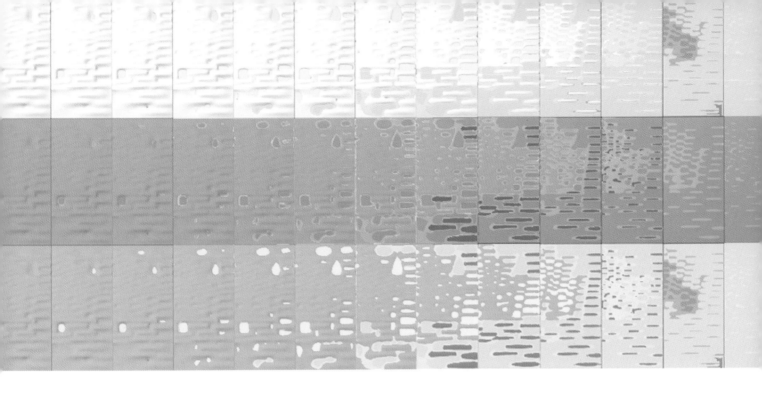

and wall. Altering the autoclave processing allows portions of the aerogel to become far denser, almost plastic in character. This stronger material, known as a xerogel but made of precisely the same materials that comprise aerogel, allows stiffening "mullions" and a "stressed skin" to be built into the material's homogeneous chemical composition. Aerogel's ability to integrate these cross-performing traits (windows that insulate or mullions that one can see through, for example) into a single material matrix confounds the tidy distinctions that we tend to assign to walls and windows.

A broader aspiration of the Ninety-eight Percent Nothing project was to enable us—a team of architects in an academic setting—to collaborate with industries and scientific agencies involved in materials research. While architecture has a rich history of collaboration with industry—Paul Rudolph and Ralph Twitchell's work with the Revere Metals Company in the early 1950s or the Case Study houses' affiliations with building prod-

ucts companies, for example—more recent materials research has been complicated by two factors. The first stems from the evolution of architectural discourse over the last five decades. The skeptical shadow cast upon canonical modernism during the last third of the twentieth century included doubts about the decidedly material ambitions that were central among modernism's tenets. The second comes from the fact that materials research tends to occur in a more rarefied context today. Much of this work takes place at the level of chemistry rather than assembly, for example, and it is often carried out in settings—in our case at Jet Propulsion Laboratory—where the potential architectural uses of these materials is less than obvious. Materials science has become a synthetic superdiscipline in which potent cross-fertilizations among chemistry, physics, engineering, economics, and material science are occurring at an ever increasing rate. New materials being synthesized through these intersections open up extraordinary possibilities for architecture's future, but they do so in settings that are easily overlooked by architects.

Aerogel

Our research began with digital models of aerogel tiles. Having determined the dimensional limits of our production abilities—tiles of approximately 7" x 7" x 1" thick—we designed a series of layered topographies whose different material compositions (clear, translucent, and opaque) were aggregated to create contoured openings across a tile and, ultimately, across a field of tiles. By placing strata of different material opacities on top of one another and across the variegated topographies of the contours, we were able to create transparent and opaque zones corresponding to the high and low geographies of the molds. In addition to creating holes in opaque surfaces and islands in clear surfaces, our contoured molds also produced a tapering of individual layers as they encountered the inflected topography of the mold. This tapering facilitated gradient transitions among the opaque and transparent areas of the tiles, thereby accentuating the material continuity of the aerogel across both its "wall" and "window" iterations.

After testing a series of topographic types, the digital mock-ups were translated into physical models. A Thermojet rapid prototyping machine was used to produce the initial physical version of each tile. These prototypes were then reverse-cast in a ceramic material to make forms that were, in turn, used to slump the undulating glass surfaces of the molds. Glass molds were required to withstand the high temperatures and high pressures of the autoclave. Once the physical mold geometries were determined and fabricated, we returned to the digital models to finalize the pouring sequences and the incremental pour depths for each of the tile types. Working digitally enabled us to verify the geometric results and the optical effects that we might anticipate in the finished tiles; it also enabled us to calculate the volume of material that would be needed for each pour.

While configuring the molding process, we focused on how a fixed mold could be used to produce variable tile types simply by changing the way in which the liquid aerogel chemistry was introduced into its volume. Used in this way, a single form produces an extraordinarily wide range of tiles through variations in the organization of clear, translucent, and opaque layers. Given the costs associated with fabricating the mold, the use of a single mold to produce a range of tile types significantly increased the economic viability of nonrepetitive production. Furthermore, while we were able to produce dozens of variants from a given mold, all belonged to one species of geometric sensibility. A tile's particular pattern of opaque and transparent areas was tethered to the shape of the mold without exactly duplicating other tiles. Thus the family of tiles generated from a specific mold relied upon both geometric configuration and material chemistry for its variant-sameness.

When arrayed across a larger surface, such as a façade, these variant-sameness tiles warrant a reconsideration of how such a surface is organized. Classical systems for proportioning façades depend upon compositional exactitude for their legibility. The syncopations of solids and voids are controlled and given legibility through the regulating lines that coincide with their centers and edges. Similarly, modern architecture's exploitation of seriality, while aimed at neutralizing hierarchies rather than pronouncing them, is equally dependent upon edges and centers to establish the parameters of a building skin's repetitive proliferation (whether in terms of a skin's appearance or its fabrication). The variant sameness of our tiles overcomes the seemingly exclusive binary of opaque (wall) and transparent (window). By optically and materially migrating each toward the other, transparent and opaque zones are rendered as same-species architectural conditions.

Resin

Our resin research elaborated the contouring/molding process across panels as large as 4' x 8.' The smaller aerogel tiles let us study the effects of aerogel layers of varying opacities as they encountered the cut-and-fill geometry of a specific mold. The larger panels allowed us to explore the modulation of cut-and-fill geometries relative to one another without the serializing constraints imposed by tiling.

As with the aerogel research, we began our resin investigation with digital models that could be directly translated into physical molds. The digital mock-ups were used to test variations in the steepness of the contours, the organization of high and low topographic zones, and, ultimately, the pour sequences that would be used during the casting process. Digital animations—in the form of sequential fill studies—were used to regulate the flow of resin into the molds, to calibrate the layer locations and thicknesses, and to determine the volume of resin that would be needed for each pour. Once the geometries of the panels were defined, the digital models were translated into styrene forms through a numerically controlled milling process. In addition to its reduction of manual labor, digital control also assured that the molds precisely conformed to the geometries of the digital studies. Given the compressed geometries that we were working with—the range of high and low points in the molds was contained within a one-inch thickness—the outcome of our research depended on the precision with which we could fabricate the molds and choreograph the placement of different layers and their respective opacities.

The most significant implications of the Ninety-eight Percent Nothing project lay in our understanding of material assembly. In its simplest terms, a conventional window is a cutout in a wall (a removal of a material) replaced with a piece of glass (a supplanting of one material with another), plus a metal or wood frame (an introduction of a third material that negotiates the two others). Our research into variant-sameness replaced this three-material system with a single-material/multigeometry system. Instead of substituting one material for another, changes in transparency, structural capacity, and thermal efficiency were produced by altering the chemical matrix of a single material. And rather than using a third material to negotiate between differing surface types, the geometries of the molds were used to link one material variant to another through the adjustable gradients of varying topographies. The hard "edges" or "centers" of openings and walls were thus translated into gradient transitions, and the compositional use of regulating lines to organize such a surface was superseded by the regulating spectra of the contoured molds. Employing material transition and geometric inflection, variant-sameness transforms the absolute certainties of optimized material performance (based on the independent definitions of walls, glazing, and mullions) into the indiscrete cohabitants of a thoroughly variegated but entirely homogeneous surface.

46

Note

A key collaborator on this project was Dr. Steven Jones, materials scientist at the Jet Propulsion Laboratory / California Institute of Technology.

An era of ultramaterials has arrived. Instead of designing according to the inherent limitations in the properties of given materials, designers can use technology to extend our capacity beyond what was once imagined possible—one can theoretically design material to meet any performance criteria. Through nanotechnology, additive coating, and surface manipulation, properties of materials are embedded and layered into the process of their fabrication. The discussion here centered around how architects can engage with ongoing scientific developments in material science; the speakers addressed the implications for the role of architects and the added responsibility that may result from this multitude of choices and possibilities.

Michael Cima My plan is to speak about some of the things I've been working on and thinking about for the past ten or fifteen years. I tell students that the thing to do while at graduate school is to work on the biggest problems they can think of. Because even if you have the wrong answer, people will still beat a path to your door if you are working on big problems.

Some of the big problems I've worked on involve the forming of shapes. There's a lot of value in shapes—I probably don't have to convince this audience of that. But many people I work with look at things through a microscope; they look at microstructure, and the properties of materials in bulk form, but they don't think necessarily of shape as the most important attribute.

Lots of times, you think of materials as being motionless. In reality, many of the materials I work with—particularly in electronics—have to move to function, or at least they're moving while we're forming them. We need to understand that motion, on a very small scale. In my research, I also study how to put materials where you really want them.

I didn't realize that you are familiar with what we call a 3-D printing process; I am one of the inventors of this process. I was involved because I work in powder technologies—forming things from powder, like ceramics. We wanted to come up with a forming technology that didn't need tooling or molds and was instead based on powders. 3-D printing relies on laminated building operations, where you'd spread layers of powder, and then ink-jet and print the glue. You end up with a bed completely filled with powder, but only certain ele-

James Carpenter Design Associates, Dichronic Light Field, 1994
Architects: Handel & Associates

ments are glued together. You reach into that powder bed and shake out the part—I think that some of you have done this with the Z-corps machine. This operation is based on ink-jet printing.

There are many different types of ink-jet printing. This is continuous ink-jet printing; high-speed ink-jet printing is another term you have heard. We make droplets at a rate of about 50,000 droplets a second for each jet on a print head. You can get these ink-jet print heads with up to 1,500—and I've heard of one with 4,500—individually controlled nozzles. Each nozzle makes 50,000 droplets a second. If you think of the data translation rate to those print heads, it is amazing. The Z-corps machine uses an off-the-shelf thermal jet printer, which is much simpler than this, but it is also slower. The future direction for this technology is not to make prototypes but to go directly into manufacturing, and the way to do that is to put larger numbers of jets to work for you.

These applications have turned into businesses that operate differently from normal businesses. Soligen is a company on the West Coast where, if you're a designer of a metal part, you send them a CAD file over the Internet. An engineer there pulls it up on his or her CAD station. They have software that automatically generates a mold with all the risers and other features that are necessary to do a casting. Then they call you back and quote a price. If you agree to that price, they have fourteen 3-D printing machines running around the clock. The mold design gets shipped over the local network and the machine builds the mold. It then goes to be fired and then to the casting division where they cast the metal part. They cut off the risers and FedEx the part back to you. These parts are usually made in five working days. Rather than just making one part, they are often making 100 parts. It is very cost-effective to do it this way, as opposed to having to make the tooling, and then make the parts.

The variation in machines and the use of 3-D printing is based on the different materials that people want to use. The Z-corps customer is more design-oriented, making prototypes. They've got a couple of different flavors of powders that are workable for design people. The other interesting new development is that the customers have been demanding color. So they just use color ink-jet print heads and you can now grade color three-dimensionally in the part. So those are some things that are happening with 3-D printing.

I want to go into another application, pharmaceutical formulations. What are the attributes of a tablet? One is the amount of drug; it has to be very specific. Another is time release: you may want the drug to go into effect instantly, or you may want it to be effective over eight hours. Stability is another important attribute: is the drug chemically stable? What if it sits on your dashboard in your car or is exposed to humidity in your bathroom?

For many therapies, you have to take multiple tablets for multiple drugs. Wouldn't it be great if you could take just one tablet and it had all the drugs in it that you need for a particular therapy? All of the attributes of the tablet are controlled by what we call the microstructure of the tablet. Tablets are not necessarily homogeneous; many of them have coatings and things like that. So there are a lot of things that are different, that would change on a 100-micron scale inside the tablet.

James Carpenter Design Associates, Phoenix Court House, 1996; Architects: Richard Meier and Partners

We thought about trying to make these dosage forms from 3-D printing. We've printed drugs into the tablet—not only the drugs but also different types of binders. If you put the tablet in water, it is going to erode from the outside inward, and the actual timed release of the drug is going to depend on where it is inside the tablet. These tablets are small, but in this application, we are going to make large numbers of tablets for it to be practical. We have a machine that makes arrays of thousands of tablets at a time—50,000 tablets an hour. The designer in this case will sit down at a CAD station and design the inside of the part, and then print it.

I am going to go onto one last topic, and that is assembly. Today we are constantly using parts that are smaller and smaller. One example is the simple chip capacitor used in electronics. The problem is that they have become so small that no one can use them because they are too small to pick up and put on a circuit board. Since you're making 6 billion a month, just think about the technology needed to put 6 billion capacitors on printed circuit boards. It's a very difficult problem. I started thinking about this in relation to the problem I had been working on. Essentially, working with powders is a lot like working with parts, especially when the parts are small. So, we've been trying to think about how one would assemble such materials.

James Carpenter Design Associates, Lichtof Façade and Roof, 1997
Architects: Muller Reismann Architekten

Jack Smith at UC-Berkeley was working on what is called the fluidic self-assembly of gallium arsenide devices. It was a very simple idea: he wanted to put all these small gallium arsenide chips on a board without having to use any work input. It turns out that the chips all have specific shapes, and the locations on the board all have a matching shape. He essentially just pours all the chips on top of a board with small features that mate with the shape of the parts. Shaking permits the parts to stochastically find their correct location. If you shake long enough, you fill all the holes and then just wipe off the excess.

Toshiko Mori To bring us back from the invisible world of nanotechnology and microscopic development, James Carpenter will discuss a collaborative course he has taught at MIT with Michael Cima. He can demonstrate for us how his work visibly manifests some of the examples of techonolgical developments in glass.

James Carpenter Michael invited me to participate in the material science department at MIT, a phenomenal place filled with professors doing extraordinary work, primarily on this micro scale. But within that same department, they also have the down-and-dirty black-smithing shop, as well as a significant facility for working with glass. In this department, there's always been a deeply founded belief that the students working on complex projects would simultaneously have the opportunity to engage with the material in a more hands-on way, as opposed to always dealing with the material through a microscope.

Some of the graduate students worked with me to try to come up with a way of dealing with the redundancy of safety within a very large glass cylindrical structure for a project in London with the architect Norman Foster. This meant trying to devise a way to work with different types of adhesives, to adhere the sleeving of glass cylinders inside each other. We did quite a few experiments in the lab, but the interest for me was really twofold. The specific project was bringing to bear not only Michael's expertise but also how the graduate students were thinking about solving a problem that I don't believe would be solved in the glass industry itself. With the exception of the float glass

process and casting technologies, the level of technology in the glass industry is relatively modest. When you want to introduce new technologies there, they're not really prepared to do so. So this was an exceptional opportunity to explore several ideas that we are continuing to develop with companies in Germany and Italy that are manufacturing these cylinders.

My specific interest is in glass composition technologies and coatings on glass, as well as working with glass as a structural material. One of the greatest problems today, in terms of how to engage with manufacturing, is that the engagement is on the level of fairly common and well-defined methodologies and production techniques, such as sheet-forming technologies or bending. There may be ways to leapfrog the current methodologies of manufacturing by actually having the materials themselves take on conforming capacities. Michael has been involved in designing glasses where you can create complex combinations of glasses, concentric rings of glasses that have varied indices of refraction, through ink-jet printing. This completely side-steps the normal thinking about how you work with glass.

Marco Steinberg If we think about architectural applications, this effort to bring industrialized techniques into architecture has been going on since the 1920s and 1930s. It has always been thought about as being the mass production of simple pieces that are then aggregated, because the simple pieces can be made in some mass-produced way.

Carpenter A fundamental thing we are talking about is that most architectural fabrication is reductive. You start with a given material —whether a 4' x 8' sheet of plywood, a 2" x 4", or a sheet of steel—and you remove that material or form it in some way. But Michael is talking about fabrication from an additive methodology, which is absolutely different.

It's a matter of not being limited by the initial product size. Currently the only architectural material that is not limited in this way is concrete. Everything else is somewhat restricted by what the given standards are, and how they have been, over time, engineered and then put into a manual such as the steel or wood handbook. All the characteristics of that material have been highly defined around

53

a series of given parts that we assemble. Using an additive methodology, you are designing from a completely different direction. You have to predetermine all those characteristics that you choose to include. And then the material will fulfill those roles. It is a totally different conceptual pattern of structure and fabrication.

Dan Schodek   The issue of scale that was brought up is also crucial in this discussion. A lot of things can be made at a terribly small scale; some things may not yet exist at useful architectural scales. Thirty-five years ago, at a materials science course at MIT, I was hearing about small fibers—called "whiskers"—with incredible tensile strengths, but at the time we didn't have an architectural application for them because they could not be made at a useful size or scale. The same remains true today—no real applications exist. Just because we can do something at the micro scale scale doesn't automatically mean that similar benefits can be easily realized at a macro scale.

Since many of these new materials and technologies operate at the micro scale and are difficult to

scale up in size, we have to be a little more thoughtful about how we use them. Just because we can develop a new light-emitting material doesn't mean that we can or should make an entire building out of it. It doesn't make sense to make a fifty-story structure out of shaped memory alloy just because we think it's cool. The issue here is how to selectively use high-end materials—how we use them intelligently, for what purpose, and where.

But how do you decide how and where to use new materials selectively or to make interventions? In many technical applications, doing so often involves thinking about the performance of whole systems to understand where to selectively intervene, and that often involves mathematical simulations. This approach implies that you don't just point over there and say, I am going to intervene at that point. You must think much more cogently. Doing so increases design complexity, and it adds value to our job. The question of where and how we selectively intervene with the use of new materials is one for the building community, the architectural community, and the product design community—not so much for the material science community.

In this same connection, I am fascinated by the idea Michael Cima discussed of selectively adding different materials for different purposes and layers; in terms of potential applications, that's an enormous area of interest for us. Our buildings typically now consist of layer upon layer of things, often seemingly glued together in some mysterious way. But I can see integrating a lot of things that we do now with separate layers directly into new materials. If we can selectively deposit different materials in different places with different characteristics, doing so could be an unbelievably powerful design technique.

Implicit in this discussion is a different way of thinking about how we select and use new synthetic and composite materials—where we design the desired properties of a material before manufacturing it (rather than our age-old process of selecting materials based on exploiting preexisting properties)— that is very innovative. But I would suggest that it puts quite an onus on us in the design process to decide what properties we want our materials to have. Many of these new materials may have a certain visual simplicity, but are also highly multifunctional. This is important in that if I want one object to do twelve things, it becomes much more complex to design the object than if I want it to do one thing. As elements become more multifunctional, it is harder to establish criteria for designing material properties to accomplish these ends, and therefore it is harder to design both the material and its method of fabrication.

I would pose a general question to Michael Cima and others in the research community of where you think these technologies are going, and how long is it going to take us to get anywhere. I think that all of us who have seen machines like the Z-corps machine downstairs immediately want to ask questions such as, "Why isn't someone trying to make a powder-based machine that does metal and other materials that has a bed of at least 50 x 50 feet?"

The issues are, of course, whether or not a technology is feasible and, if so, how long does it take a frontier technology to actually get into use. Pharmaceutical companies like to emphasize how long it takes and how much it costs to go from a drug concept to something that

gets prescribed by your doctor. They cite something like twelve to fifteen years and up to half a billion dollars. But when I talk to a lot of material scientists, they say that this time estimate is probably optimistic; it often takes twenty or thirty years for new materials to become common in the marketplace.

Cima Twenty years is typical. Teflon is one example. Teflon was invented around 1940. I think it had classified uses during World War II, but no major commercial uses until the late 1960s or so.

Schodek I remember the introduction of now commonplace plumbing pipes made out of PVC. There were big practical problems in introducing this material into the building industry. All of the major building codes throughout the country initially refused to accept it. The resistance had nothing to do with the performance characteristics of the material, of course; it had to do with the existing labor structure. People invested in traditional materials, people who specialized in working with cast iron pipe—were they going to lose their jobs? It took many years before major changes were introduced into the building codes to allow PVC to be used in this seemingly simple application.

Mori Going back to the process of material development, another innovation is the speed with which multiple and complex tasks are combined and simultaneously embedded in the material itself. How do you accelerate that process?

Cima It depends on what you are trying to build. In our case, in moving individual particles around, we wanted to assemble a part of something. And you're dealing with micron-size particles. To do that in real time, and in a reasonable amount of time, you have to place particles at the megahertz frequency rate. You have to think of ways that the assembly is going to go on at a microscopic scale and ways that everything can happen at the same time; that's the general rule that we found. We started with printing, for example, with the concept of purely prototyping, and speed wasn't an issue. It was really by luck that the technologies out there allowed us to do things in parallel. You never get an ink-jet printer with just one jet. Even a desk-jet has fifty. So, it's parallelism—that's the way to do it.

Mori Parallelism is a very powerful new paradigm. It is analogous to the recent, gradual shift in the mode of production in architecture. The way we foresee the future of building activity is in a collaborative, parallel manner, where architects, engineers, and contractors work together. Because the only way we can save time and therefore money is to change the manner of working from a pyramidal and linear mode to a parallel tasking mode.

Nader Tehrani The way that I think of building a building is often more sequential: one crew comes in, they do their work; then the electricians come in, and then the plumbers arrive. They have to do things in sequence, as opposed to parallel.

Mori Well, we're wondering if we always have to do it that way. (laughter)

Cima That's why I want to invite all my electrician friends to see this new way of fabricating structures; where a wall might be fabricated with electrical, plumbing, and other services built simultaneously within its structure. In other words, when we assemble the walls, the electrical is already there.

Mori This thinking process of how to accelerate self-assembly does filter down into how we think about a new concept model for the future of the building process.

Ivan Amato If you can come up with self-assembly processes, or any other kind of synthesizing methods that build in multiple functions, then you don't have to bring in different crews to provide the different functions you need in a building; the material itself is multifunctional. As we were talking about before, it sounds like this methodology would affect society in many ways.

One interesting vision for the smart materials angle would be to build in monitoring functions of a building's condition. You wouldn't have to put it in every square millimeter of a building, just in very pivotal points where stresses and strains are greatest. You could imagine doing this in every important point in an entire city, with, say, fiber-optic sensors that can keep track of stresses and strains, temperature, and chemical environments—all feeding into a kind of central monitoring system. Then you can do much more targeted maintenance in the city, which would save taxpayers a lot of money. There are

some smart materials folks who would want to take that vision even further, and put in self-healing properties. There are actually a few examples in the powder world, and in the cement world, of self-healing kinds of materials.

Mori After meeting the criteria for behavior, performance over time and maintenance become the issue. If we can combine these properties, we can truly create invincible materials. How does one cope with the highly calibrated and complex production of such materials?

Cima One of the problems with machining—a subtractive process—is that complexity costs you. The more complicated the shape is, the more tool paths you have to plan, and the more cutting you have to do. With additive processes it takes the same amount of time to make a block as it does to make a complicated shape. So while that bed may have a thousand parts in it, each of those parts can be different. Those parts are being made simultaneously. It has absolutely no impact on the productivity of the system.

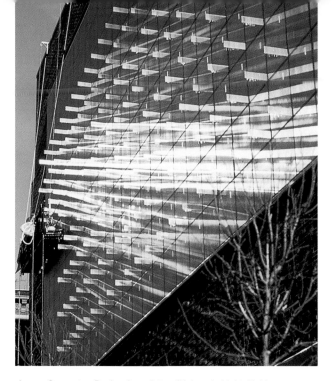

James Carpenter Design Associates, Dichronic Light Field, 1994
Architects: Handel & Associates

I believe that many of the problems we have described can be addressed by utilizing a construction method where complexity comes at no cost —that is, construction methods where making a complex object is no more difficult than making a box. The only differential in cost will be the design effort put into new elements.

Mori Once it is invented, what path does it take to arrive at the point of actual use?

Schodek I find that people hesitate to specify new materials for two main reasons: first, how long do they perform? Second are environmental concerns: how are the materials going to affect the health of people?

Cima Another problem in introducing new materials is accounting for the change in properties that occurs over long periods of time. To test them, you have to wait twenty years to determine whether the material will suffer significant degradation. The form of testing depends on whether you're talking about a mechanical property, or an optical property, or all of these things. That's what my colleagues do: they study ways to predict the performance of materials in extreme environments. One of those extremes is time; another is use. That is why it can take twenty years to introduce a new material.

Mori One way of accelerating the adoption of environmental thinking into materials innovation, manufacturing, processing, and use can actually come from the policy level; those who make materials, or who use those materials and products, can be made responsible for what happens to those products after their useful life. I think Germany has been leading in this area. If you make a car in Germany, are you not responsible for it after its use? And that brings in all kinds of pressures for manufacturers to really think seriously about the product life cycle.

Audience Those comments start to illustrate that a building can be seen as a high-performance structure. A building is such a compound relational structure. How can we start to optimize the building in its entire assembly? How do we avoid repeating the same structure over and over again, while optimizing the parts? Perhaps we should investigate optimizing the whole? Maybe even making some components obsolete in the evolution of it? Are there other industries that look into these relationships?

57

Cima   The aircraft industry was trying—the trade-offs there are immense. Any time you change a material in one place, the weight distribution in the plane changes, and all of these things are tied together in very complex, nonlinear ways.

Carpenter   I'm going to reference this subject in terms of the glass industry; glass is actually a highly sophisticated material with numerous types of coatings that affect performance and provide greater transparency and thermal benefits. Many of those advances, I would say, have been driven as much by failures as by intent. The primary example being here in Boston with the Hancock Tower, which ultimately transformed the technologies and the methodology of coating and sealing glass systems. The glass compositions and configurations that we now use are very sophisticated products.

Tehrani   It's just an amazing opportunity. Because we no longer have any restraints. It's sort of like we can design anything. We can make the stuff to do what we want. That's a terrible crisis.

Mori   We talked about the role of designers in this whole process. The possibility that designers would actually affect the process of manufacturing and design the process of fabrication is interesting. Do you have some examples?

Cima   Close to eight years ago I was at Boeing, talking about aircraft design. An aircraft fuselage is sort of cigar-shaped, and the inside plastic shell is hung on the structural frame on the outside with little tabs, and each tab has a different shape. Those tabs are bent sheet metal, made in a form— a hardened steel tool. A group of designers were designing the computer engineering code to predict the right shape of this hardened steel tool, but they then realized that it would be easier and cheaper to produce the tools as needed. Every time they want to produce a bracket, they can just pull a block of aluminum off the shelf, cut the tool for the part they're going to make that day, and then recycle the aluminum. They did an economic model for the whole process and realized that this is vastly less expensive than using a hardened tool because of the complexity and cost of inventorying such expensive pieces. This is a case where the designer radically changed the

idea of what materials they use in the fabrication process and how they think about their production of airplanes. To make tooling as needed, as opposed to making one set of tools that is permanently in the inventory.

Mori   That is a wonderful example, because it addresses the effects of details on the entire holistic picture of the production line.

Jamie Carpenter, you design, fabricate, and install your projects. Do all of the various stages of processes inform and influence each other?

Carpenter   The only reason we've been driven to enter into the construction phase of the work is that there was not anyone willing to assume the risk. Just by wanting to accomplish some of these things, we entered into it ourselves.

Michael, in particular, has been talking about composite materials in the sense of particle aggregations. The extension of what he's discussing is that you could produce a wall section that is weathertight, thermally sufficient, electroconductive, structural, etc. You could very easily envision one of

58

these ink-jet machines operating on site. It is basically building the building without the sequential services of plumbers and all that.

But this raises the question: do we want that? (laughter) If all these things are possible, do we not want to step back into this world of tectonics? We're dealing with the interfaces between materials and the junctures that create architecture; how far do you want to go? Is that really what people are after? This is coming back to your first point. What are you asking of the behavior of the material?

Schodek Let's assume that somehow we wanted to do all these amazing things. . . Let's assume that we did have some objective like that—to aggressively develop applications and architecture. Progress then has to do with the sponsorship of innovation and how innovation occurs. And where does money come from? We always look at different fields jealously. We see the fact that other research has applications in the health, aerospace, and automotive industries. There's a lot of money floating around these industries and potential sponsorship of innovative work, because there's a payoff. But I look at our own field and wonder where and how innovations get sponsored. I see a little work going on in companies—not much in terms of product development—but I see some nice high-end buildings. The value of the building warrants an investment in something very special.

Cima I have a long-standing relationship with the 3-M Corporation. I work specifically with a business unit called "Industrial Mineral Products." Their primary output is the colored rocks that go into asphalt shingles. (laughter) You can create optical effects that make an asphalt shingle roof look like a slate roof, which is enabled by the color in the rock. They add a great deal of value with both the palette of colors and the controllability of the color: each lot is exactly the same color. A lot of high-tech know-how went into getting all of those colors and making sure that they're the same.

Mori So you'd use a very practical, mundane, and widely used application to support and promote your innovative research work?

Cima Yes.

Amato A recent example of research funding is the national nanotechnology initiative, which just succeeded in getting through the machinery of government to the tune of $423 million. A coalition of people interested in getting a lot of money got together and drummed up a legitimate PR machine. I wrote one of the documents that went into the package that went to Congress and the appropriate committees. I was in a meeting where economic advisors to the president were talking to leaders of national laboratories who were part of this coalition, coaching them on how to do the pitch.

If you can make buildings that are more comfortable, that are more environmentally sound—that have lots of better properties than they do now—then you might have an argument that governments would listen to.

59

phenomena

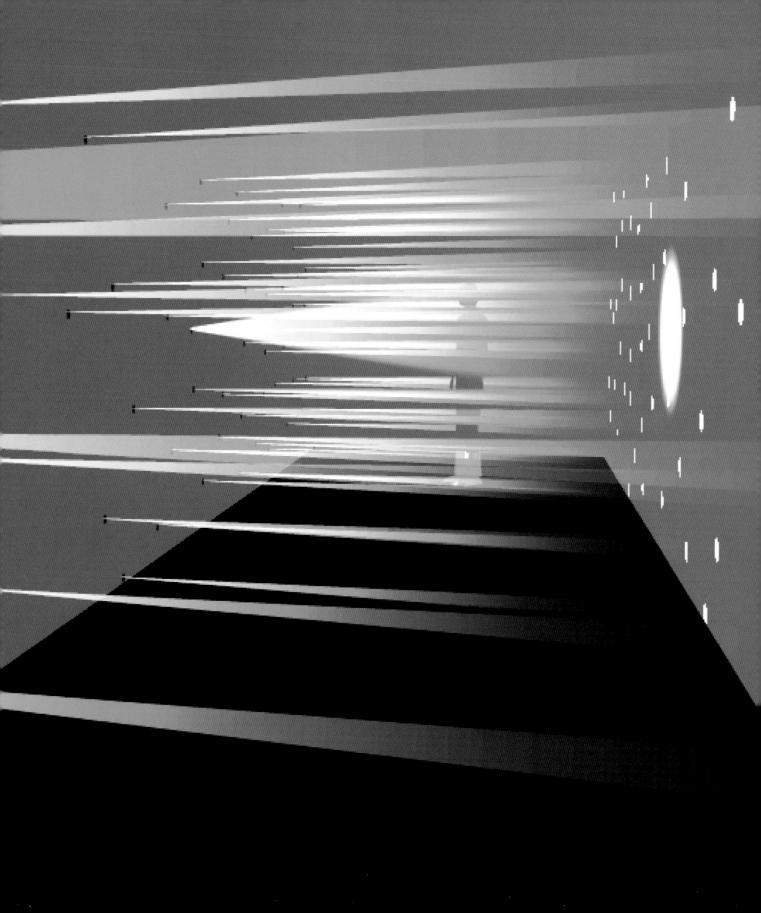

phenomena

TOSHIKO MORI

Within the discourse of materiality, how material characteristics are perceived through the human senses is an inevitable subject for research. In a world of virtual reality and simulation, desensitization is depriving us of a wealth of information that lies beyond surface visual and verbal cognition. We predict that the development of innovative materials must take place in parallel with new approaches to engaging human senses. Targeted appeals to the tactile, auditory, and olfactory senses, as well as to vision, will provide increased awareness of the many subtle messages that surround us.

We included the following materials in our research: foam, felt, paint, coatings, light, sound, and smell. Some of these are tangible materials, and others are not. Foam is a tactile material that responds to body position and weight; it uses air as an agent to reduce the bulk of substance used in its manufacture. This air enables foam to absorb sound, heat, cold, moisture, and impact, which gives it great potential as an insulation material. Felt, a reconstituted material made of recycled wool, is also highly absorbent and therefore also insulates. Paint, film, and other coatings create thin layers that can transform the original materials to which they are applied. A simple surface application can change optical properties, insulating possibilities, and even structural strength. The performance of these surface layerings can be enhanced through molecular manipulation and nanotechnology.

The thinness of these materials becomes a virtue and facilitates possible results that cannot be attained with thick materials.

By creatively lighting surfaces, for example, many psychological effects can be achieved that subtly transform mundane environments. Fiber-optic lights, in particular, project precise shadows to reveal hidden structure as well as illuminate the texture of surfaces. Fiber optics conserve energy with their low ambient lighting levels, yet their selective placement of light encourages the viewer to focus on the lit object. Similarly, sound and scent can perform, inform, and transform; their impact is strongly felt even in the absence of a material artifact in the traditional sense, making them some of the most efficient "immaterials" for use by designers. (Imagine, for example, being able to codify boundaries and thresholds without built walls or other hard structures.)

We layered these sensory elements onto our affiliated research into tangible materials such as recycled paper–based fiberboard and aerogel (see descriptions of these projects, this volume). A sound installation in a prototype space constructed of this fiberboard, for example, played recorded ambient office sounds such as shuffling paper, photocopy machines, and computer keyboards; these sounds resonated within the hollowness of the fiberboard wall, with the muffled effect implying the acoustical properties of the wall material.

An interactive virtual barrier activated by passers-by announced the fragility of aerogel by playing the recorded sound of the material. A foam bench specified its boundary by emitting sounds audible only to those sitting on it and leaning against the adjacent wall;

sounds were transmitted that vibrated through the wall's surface and into the body itself. This foam bench also interacted with passers-by with a refracting focused light spectrum, which created multicolored shadows against the wall when people interfered with the light spectrum. The bench thus performed multiple roles as a tactile artifact (foam), reactive material (temperature-sensitive paint), audible element (sound installation), and light-interactive agent (light installation). The bench exemplified a simplicity and integrity of materials yet displayed a complexity of functions and interactions as experienced by various senses.

architecture smells

METTE AAMODT

Sight, sound, and touch are the primary means by which we understand form, space, and materials. But what do the polished marble, urethane-coated wood, and hot-rolled steel in Alvaro Siza's buildings smell like? How do the resins, solvents, and pigments in latex paint, or gypsum-based plaster and drywall, or nylon carpets and epoxy carpet glues affect our perception of the spaces we inhabit? How much can we understand about a space from its smell?

Smells can give us information about who occupies a space, what activities occur there, and what materials are used. At a time when new materials are being researched and created, and common materials applied in new ways, can smell be considered a viable "material" for architecture?

The sense of smell has a powerful connection with memory and emotions, and represents an untapped potential for our experience and perception of architecture. Through smell we can create a language of recognition, or perception through association. Odors catalog significant memories in the brain, and those memories are involuntarily recalled when a person comes into contact with the smell again, thereby collapsing the space and time between the two events. Whether the memory is recalled five years after the initial event or twenty-five years later makes no difference; smell memory, unlike visual memory, does not fade with time.

By exploiting all of the senses, it is possible to create a multilayered experience that evokes a transparency of time, space, memory, and feeling. As Maurice Merleau-Ponty observed, "My perception is not a sum of visual, tactile, and audible givens: I perceive in a total way with my whole being: I grasp a unique structure of a thing, a unique way of being, which speaks to all of my senses at once."[1] In western culture, however, seeing has always held a preeminent position because it is the primary means by which we acquire knowledge. In fact, 90 percent of all information is received by our eyes and sent to the left hemisphere of the brain, where conscious thought is processed. As Martin Heidegger noted, "Even in the early stages of Greek philosophy, and not by accident, cognition was conceived in terms of the 'desire to see.'"[2] In our culture's search for truth, the eyes have been given primacy, for "seeing is believing." Western architecture has been greatly influenced by Plato, who considered sight and hearing to be the noble senses because they put us in contact with the world of perfection—geometry and music—not the physical world of touch and smell.

Yet animals rely more on their sense of smell than on their vision to orient themselves in space, to mark territory, to trigger mating behavior, and to guide themselves to food sources. Humans have only a fraction of the olfactory receptors that animals do (10 million in humans versus 1 billion in dogs); olfaction, however, is still an integral part of the way we experience the

The olfactory system catalogs smells in the brain according to their associations. When an unfamiliar smell is detected, the body assumes a state of alert until the nature of the smell can be recorded. When a familiar smell is detected, the brain performs a search of its memory to recognize it. Vladimir Nabokov referred to odor memory in his novel *Mary*: "Memory can restore to life everything but smells, although nothing revives the past so completely as a smell that was once associated with it."[3] The smell acts as a trigger—the memory of a significant episode includes only the experiences of the other senses and related emotions, not the smell itself. In architecture, would it be possible to create a heightened emotional atmosphere by manipulating smells that act on the subconscious? Or what if, by making a new smell, the "space" of a building was extended by association?

Until recently little was known about how the olfactory system works. In fact, even today we do not know what properties of odor molecules are associated with their smell. There is no relationship for odor like there is for color between wavelength and color perception, or for sound between frequency and pitch. Negative associations and cultural taboos surrounding smell have impeded much serious scientific investigation.

Whereas sight has been linked with the intellect, smell has been associated with primitive instincts, sex, disease, and decay. The Egyptians enjoyed the erotic pleasures of perfumes and used them for ritualistic offerings. Plato, on the other hand, considered odors to be vulgar and feminine. At the time of the Enlightenment, Romantics like Rousseau praised emotion, smell, and eroticism, while others believed that "as the sense of lust, desire and impulse [smell] carries with it the stamp of animality."[4] Medical diagnosis in the nine-

world. The olfactory system in humans is evolutionarily one of the oldest parts of the brain, and smell is the first sense to emerge during fetal development. The olfactory bulb, located at the top of the nasal passage, contains receptors that are in direct contact with the air we breath. This outcropping of the brain is connected to the limbic system, which plays an important role in perception and memory, as well as emotions and motivation. If the sense of smell provides a direct neurological link between our physical environment and our feelings, moods, and memories, does that not have an impact on how we perceive, understand, and relate to architecture?

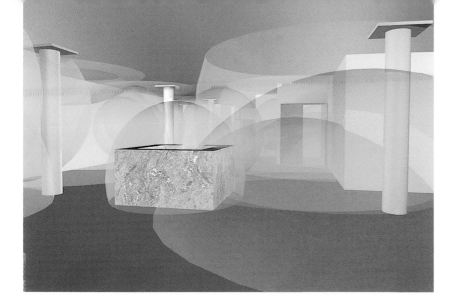

teenth century was almost entirely predicated on the odors given off by different parts of the body. Rancid smells in the city were considered deadly, and sickness was attributed to bad air, or miasma, which led to a century of urban and architectural improvements aimed at eliminating these bad odors.

The taboos surrounding smell are pervasive and have found their way into the aesthetic discourse of architecture. Sanitary and hygiene reforms of the nineteenth century originated out of a desire to eliminate odors, which were considered carriers of disease. During the plague, doctors were said to have protected themselves from disease by holding a sachet of potpourri under their noses. Similarly, streets were paved and hospital walls whitewashed to stop the gases that were thought to be emanating from them. Stone, plaster, and paint were used to create a hermetic surface that not only acted as a deodorizer but also provided the appearance of cleanliness. Rudolph el-Khoury has argued that the modern surface is the extension of a visual logic of cleanliness, and that the universal appeal of the white wall in modern architecture arises from its ability to translate odorlessness into an image. "Olfactory vigilance ultimately served to reorganize the environment according to the dialectic of transparency and opacity that shaped the *aesthetic* of cleanliness."[5]

The flat white walls of modern architecture represent a desire to convey abstract concepts and ideas rather than sensory experiences. The move away from sensual materials, what Juhani Pallasmaa calls "matter," toward mute surfaces has meant the elimination of a vast repository of associations that once served to give places their personality and meaning.[6] As Ivan Illich observed, "Unlike the architect who constructed a palace to suit the aura of his wealthy patron, the new architect constructed shelter for a yet unidentified resident who was supposed to be without odor."[7]

Bernard Tschumi has also taken issue with the false split between the realm of the mind and the reality of spatial experience in architecture by targeting cultural taboos like decay and the erotic as the means for transcending this paradox. The pure white structures of the 1930s embodied society's fears of death and decay, and an admiration for the dry white ruins of antiquity. But architecture, he argues, can exist only by embracing "the pleasure of excess." "Architecture is the ultimate erotic act. Carry it to excess and it will reveal both the traces of reason and the sensual experience of space."[8]

In 1949 Richard Neutra wrote: "We must guard against the notion that the only sense perceptions which really count are those which are easily and consciously perceived. On the contrary, one might say that an environmental influence may be particularly pernicious where the consciousness does not correct it. We should therefore pay full attention—and future experimentation will undoubtedly do so—to all of the non-visual aspects of architectural environment and design."[9] His expectation that subsequent generations would take up these issues has so far not been realized. We should not overlook the fact that architecture smells, and that that smell is a potential material to be used to its greatest advantage. Smell can be used to imbue richness to surfaces, to define zones and boundaries, and to create powerful associations that can give greater meaning to spaces and buildings. Babylonian temples smelled sweet from the perfume used in their mortar; why do our concrete monuments only smell of Portland cement?

My initial investigations of smell have been in terms of its relationship to memory and the powerful link that a single smell can create between multiple spaces, experiences, and moments. A concrete wall, if infused with a recognizable odor, could act as a screen onto which memory is projected. The cinematic quality of this scenario is an analogy for the collapse of the two spaces—the space of the initial event and the space where the event has been recalled—and demonstrates how smell can be used to create a greater transparency of space and time.

My research investigated how smell can be used to give greater perceptual depth to architecture. I designed a gypboard surface, constructed away from an existing wall, with a niche cut out for a seat. The niche was lined on either side with thick gray felt infused with lilac oil. Head and seat cushions were installed, and a single piece of felt was draped over them, creating the gentle curve of the back. The felt surfaces absorbed not only the lilac scent but also much of the ambient sound, and the soft, wooly texture provided a warm and comfortable enclosure. The gypboard was painted with a pale iridescent paint that refracted a spectrum of colors from a fiber-optic lighting system installed in the ceiling. Lighting was also used to create a visual association with the lilac smell by adding a zone of purple light above the seat.

The seat provided a resting place where a person could pause and take time to experience the scent in the felt walls of the niche. Some people recognized the smell as lilac, a flower commonly found in New England in the spring, but many could only say what they were reminded of. In this private space, one was free to recall memories and make associations, or, at the very least, relax and be comfortable. The unusual appearance of this smell in late winter would, I hoped, have the effect of triggering memories that would transport people for an instant—to another place, another time, another season—and collapse the two episodes, giving greater perceptual depth to the space.

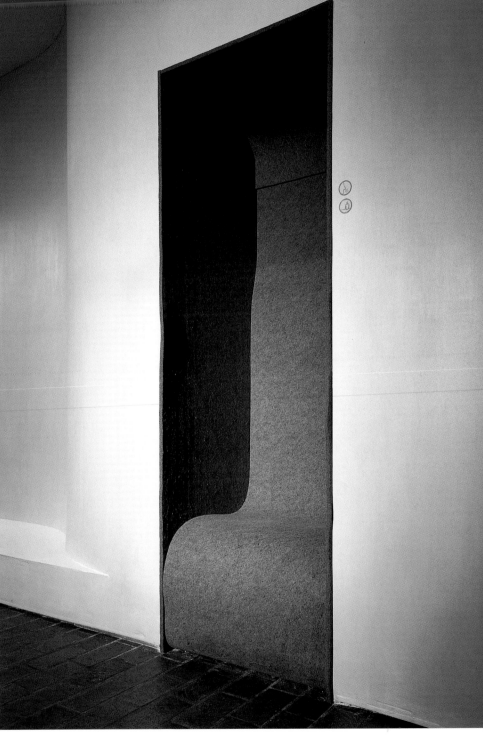

Notes

1. Quoted in Juhani Pallasmaa, "Hapticity and Time—Notes on a Fragile Architecture," *Architectural Review* (May 2000), 78.

2. Martin Heidegger, *Being and Time* (Albany: State University of New York Press, 1996), 160.

3. Quoted in Trygg Engen, *Odor Sensation and Memory* (New York: Praeger, 1991), 6.

4. Piet Vroon, *Smell: The Secret Seducer* (New York: Farrar, Straus, and Giroux, 1994), 8.

5. Rudolph el-Khoury, "Polish and Deodorize: Paving the City in Late Eighteenth-Century France," *Assemblage* 31 (December 1996), 10.

6. Pallasmaa, 79.

7. Ivan Illich, *H_2O and the Waters of Forgetfulness* (Berkeley: Heyday Books, 1985), 54.

8. Bernard Tschumi, "Architecture and Transgression," *Oppositions Reader,* ed. K. Michael Hays (New York: Princeton Architectural Press, 1998), 36.

9. Richard Neutra, "The Sound and Smell of Architecture," *Progressive Architecture* (November 1949), 65.

body, performance, boundary

TALA KLINCK

Engaged in perpetual motion, the living body is essentially a continuous sequence of kinesthetic responses, a sensitive and expressive organism that moves in relation to time and situation. The materials that surround the human body, including clothing and shelter, function as boundaries that mediate between the body and its environment. While these boundaries protect the body, they also function to express its activity by either accentuating or hiding its transformations. The spaces between the boundaries are architectures, ranging in scale from the most intimate—the space between skin and clothing—to the most grand—the space between body and building. The body or bodies that inhabit these spaces animate them with their "everyday life, movement and action."[1]

This indicates the potential for an architecture that emphasizes the dynamic quality of materials—perhaps an architecture defined not by permanent partitions but by dynamic boundaries that choreograph movement by engaging and responding to human activity.

Traditionally boundaries have been understood as thresholds that divide one space from another—the inner from the outer, or the private from the public. Dynamic boundaries, on the other hand, do not just divide two entities; they are entities themselves, and they may lie within a single space. They respond to human activity and even require human interference to function. By either triggering or inhabiting these boundaries, the people who move through them also define them. Space is therefore shaped and choreographed by the kinesthetic response of the human body.

Fashion designer Issey Miyake emphasizes this dialogue between the body and material. Speaking about his work, he explains, "From the beginning I thought about working with the body in movement, the space between the body and clothes. I wanted the clothes to move when people moved. The clothes are also for people to dance or laugh."[2] His clothing demonstrates "a co-existence of cloth and body which become one through movement."[3] The body animates the clothing, which reshapes the body, which moves the clothes, and so on.

Yet obviously the human body does not respond only to visual media; it also responds to touch, smell, and sound. In the words of Juhani Pallasmaa, "The task of architecture is to make visible how the world touches us,"[4] and this requires a haptic architecture that considers not one but all of the senses. It also requires us to reconsider how boundaries are designated. A boundary can be as thin as a line or as thick as a space, and matter of any density can create *poche*. This includes gases, liquids, and solids, or any combination of the three.

Many modern architectures exhibit materials that evoke an unrealistic perpetual present. In attempt to construct permanent visual and physical boundaries, they deny the passing of time and the effects of use. According to Pallasmaa, by prioritizing shape and volume, "form is vocal, whereas matter is mute."[5]

In our research, we created dynamic boundaries by giving voice to matter. Boundaries of sound, smell, light, and tactile surfaces engage people in an improvisational dialogue through which they actively choreograph space. Sounds and smells refer to spaces in the past, bring near spaces that are far away, and magnify spaces too small for the human body to inhabit. Walking through a prototypical passageway made of fiberboard, for example, one heard the taped sounds of the space's construction. Tactile surfaces including foam, felt, paper, and rubber collapsed the space between skin and boundary, and fiber-optic lighting added emphasis to the qualities inherent in the materials.

Touch, sound, and light all contributed to making the effects of a specially designed bench, for instance, more significant than its simple physical form might suggest. Soft "memory" foam, inlaid into the rigid polyurethane structure of the bench, invited people to sit within the periphery of the space. Leaning against the wall behind the bench revealed the sounds of congested traffic from another time and place. Colored fiber optics, embedded in the bench, provided the only light in the area. The lights focused on the opposite wall as circles of seemingly white light, but when passers-by interfered with these boundaries, their shadows registered on the wall as bright colors. The shadows of seated people appeared large and somewhat indistinct compared to the sharply rendered shadows of people passing through the space. The space was mute and empty until human activity disrupted the equilibrium and revealed the hidden colored composition that changed with each moment.

Thus the construction of dynamic boundaries alludes to an architecture that is both formless and haptic, an architecture that, like the body, transforms over time and constantly encounters new spaces. Most important, it provides the opportunity for architects to imply rather than dictate choreography.

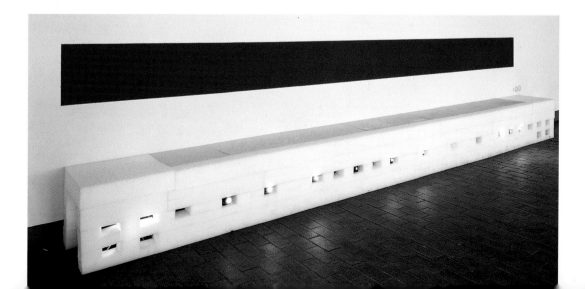

Notes

1. Bernard Tschumi, *Architecture and Disjunction* (Cambridge, MA: MIT Press, 1998).

2. Joan Simon, "Miyake Moder," *Art in America* (February 1999).

3. Ibid.

4. Juhani Pallasmaa, *The Eyes of the Skin* (London: Academy Editions, 1996), 78.

5. Ibid., 79.

ephemeral light

SHOZO TOYOHISA

translated by Mark Mulligan and Hiroto Kobayashi

My work focuses on how to realize—in concrete terms—the light responding to an architect's image of a space. I am always thinking of how light can express a kind of human language. For me, lighting design is never a matter of simply allocating light from standard manufactured fixtures; instead, I believe in a more hand-crafted approach to lighting design that has the potential to affect people more directly. In my design process, I fabricate everything from a single recessed can light to original fixtures designed for a variety of architectural spaces. In terms of the actual technique of making this hand-crafted light, I always attempt to harness the very latest technology as much as possible. While developing new techniques for my lighting, I also incorporate technology from many other related fields. My reason for using the latest technology for this hand-crafted light is that the newer the lighting technology, generally speaking, the less it stands out in the space. In other words, my idea is to make the actual fixture as invisible as possible so that the focus of the design is just the light required for each space.

Let me explain with a few recent examples. I will begin with the case of the Gallery of Horyu-ji Treasures of the Tokyo National Museum, which opened in July 1999. The 300 or so artifacts assembled in this pavilion are about 1,200 years old and are among the most important national treasures of Japan; they include many items that present extreme difficulties for preservation. The treasures are placed in permanent exhibition, which means that the most stringent preservation measures were required for the lighting design. While responding to these very pragmatic requirements, I also needed to address the architect's design concept of recreating a kind of 1,200-year-old light. For this, I decided to search for clues as to what that 1,200-year-old light would look like. Then one day it hit me—I thought about the recent influx of Buddhism to Japan from China during that time and how the people who originally visited the Horyu-ji Temple in Nara would have seen these works in what must have been the dim light of the temple interiors. Confronting images of the Buddha while taking in the impressions of the entire space must have inspired a kind of unique spiritual landscape in their hearts. If I wanted to recreate the light of 1,200 years ago, it was not really a matter of pursuing the physical light source itself but rather of recreating this internal, spiritual landscape, using today's technology—this idea became the basis of my project design.

To understand the design problem more fully, I actually began studying Buddhism and conversing with the people who live and work in these temples. I visited temples many times until I began to feel intuitively the direct correspondence of light and Buddhist space. Therefore, my design process became a matter of translating these experiences into individual moments of the museum interior. If we think about it, the Japanese have had from ancient times a heightened sensibility for light and shadow in architecture—as the author Jun'ichiro Tanizaki has expressed in his well-known essay "In Praise of Shadows," for example. Probably my own childhood and education in such an environment has made it possible for me to realize my work in lighting design this way. In any case, that explains a bit my thoughts behind this design—but in terms of how the work then progressed from idea to physical resolution, I responded to the museum's request to create beautiful light by developing light fixtures with halogen bulbs at their core. Taking advantage of the latest research of Phillips laboratories, we were able to produce a fixture that could be naturally ventilated and cooled, therefore eliminating ambient noise.

In devising my lighting strategy, I assumed that the idea of shining a halogen light directly on the works on exhibition would never be approved for reasons of preservation science. So I used optical cables of glass fiber to transmit light from the light source to the works. Along the way it was possible to filter out damaging ultraviolet rays (all frequencies smaller than 400 nanometers are removed); similarly, infrared rays are completely removed by passing this light through a dichronic glass filter. Thus not only were the museum's technical problems resolved but the lighting devices in the room could be extremely small—producing a serene architectural space while providing a high-quality light that perfectly preserves the artifacts on display.

Next I will mention the Prada Beauty project, which began in 2000. The Prada company wanted to associate its line of cosmetics with a prominent shop, and for its interior they desired an environment that would glow with clean, soft light, making women appear beautiful. Beginning with this request and the design concept of Prada's architect Kazuyo Sejima, I thought about making all the light in the shop indirect, reflecting off interior wall surfaces. I designed some original museum-grade wall washer fixtures provided with three-dimensional reflectors to cleanly illuminate the joint between wall and ceiling and to scatter the light perfectly evenly, without shadows. The absence of ordinary shadows makes the room appear full of light. Visitors to the store are able to try out the cosmetics in this beautiful diffuse-light environment, and so far they have been very satisfied.

The final project I want to discuss is the entrance pavilion to the Tokyo subway station at Roppongi 1-chome, an example where the lighting fixture itself was to become a focus in the architectural design. All illumination for the pavilion's transparent glass volume is provided by a single fixture in the center. The fixture is made of a large-diameter tube of transparent polycarbonate whose inner surface is coated with an optical lens film. Light enters the tube from sources at both ends and escapes through the tube's sides to produce an evenly scattered light for the space. At night, the fixture

Shozo Toyohisa, Lighting Designer, Tokyo National Museum, Gallery of Horyu-ji Treasures, 1999; Architects: Taniguchi & Associates

appears to passers-by as a huge, symbolically glowing pipe. But rather than producing the unpleasant glare of ordinary fluorescent lights, this glowing tube produces a more subtle glow that seems futuristic in its sense of transparency. The transparent glass volume and its transparent lamp produce a kind of liberating effect on the street environment at night.

These are my most recent major projects. Though each one is different, they all represent a search for light's spiritual qualities—an attempt to produce a light environment that suggests a spiritual landscape. Certainly each time I begin a problem, I equip myself with the latest technology. At the same time, I am not at all interested in showing off technology for its own sake; my aim is to raise my work to the level where the technique is no longer noticed.

One of my current projects is an art museum whose lighting fixtures will be housed behind a 1"-wide slit in the ceiling surface. Though the lamps will be precisely aimed to illuminate works on the museum walls, the visual presence of the lighting fixtures will be completely erased from the room, allowing visitors to concentrate on appreciating the art. For the future, I am also looking into using things like light-emitting diodes (LEDs) as an essential light source that might be precisely manipulated through digital controls. I believe it might be possible eventually to change the way we think about the expression of light, relating it more directly to human experience.

Jacques Herzog had just been awarded, with his partner Pierre de Meuron, the 2001 Pritzker Prize in architecture when he participated in this discussion at the Graduate School of Design. Moderator Toshiko Mori and other participants sought to elicit Herzog's personal perspective about materiality and his thoughts on the larger question, "What is architecture?" Following are excerpts from this discussion.

Left and Below: Herzog & de Meuron, Prada Shop and Offices, Tokyo

Toshiko Mori   In *Technics and Civilization*, published in 1934, Lewis Mumford characterized the evolving use of power and material in machine-age production as following distinct phases: eotechnic, which involves water and wood; paleotechnic, using coal and iron; and neotechnic, based on electricity and alloys. Now we are facing material development and production processes based on molecular chemistry and light—involving nanotechnology—which may be less tectonic, less articulate. Yet these factors have an amazing effect on performance. In all of architecture today, your work with Pierre de Meuron presages such a new age. Your preoccupation with continuous and dynamic surfaces implies the absence of joinery; a continuity of surfaces is achieved in your work, within the limitations of the current building industry, which raises the possibility of different types of techniques and tectonics.

If you were to characterize your approach to material exploration, would you say that aesthetics interacts visually with phenomena and the technical performance of materials? Or does the technical become subordinated, as opposed to the expression of technical articulation in high-tech architecture? Conceptually, your buildings produce a mysterious and seductive effect; your work often resembles that of contemporary conceptual artists rather than architects, because the work is almost a meditation and a reflection of our time and our civilization. Your body of work also reflects the relationships of light and materials. Therefore I cannot but assume that your and Pierre's architecture signals your profound interest in materiality.

Jacques Herzog   It does not signal a profound interest in materials as such. It does, however, signal a profound interest in the physical world. Everything is physical; even our thoughts are developed, transferred, and communicated in a physical body. If we want to know more about the world behind or beyond that physical world, we have to deal with its very physical and material conditions.

This is an old story, a very old story. The history of human culture could be written on the basis of the dialectics of material versus immaterial—the history of religions, of philosophy, of natural and social sciences, of art and, of course, also of architecture. Take German Romanticism of the nineteenth century as an example of an almost alchemist perception of the world versus attempts in abstract painting —specifically by American painters of the twentieth century such as Barnett Newman, or more radically even, Ad Reinhart—to eliminate all traces of figuration, of production, of materiality. We feel affinities to both attitudes—the Romantic position as well as the abstract one. If you look back in history at all these attempts to produce works of art, of architecture, of literature, it's always a struggle with the physical givens of our *condition humaine*, a struggle to transcend them, to reach something else, and ultimately to understand the

world, to understand who and what we are. The work of Herzog and de Meuron is as much about immaterials as about materials—it deals with the paradox of our physical world.

Mori   Maybe you could talk a bit about some ways in which you enhance ordinary materials. I'm interested in the way you work with artists, in terms of inscribing materials, and how, for example, concrete panels or glass transforms into something more. As you say, they gain more of a Romantic surface quality as a result, with images associated with them—and textures.

Herzog   Take the balcony in this auditorium as an example. It's a concrete beam that is painted all over. This is perhaps the worst way to use materials, lacking all consciousness and intellectual awareness. The concrete as a material is hidden, it plays no active role; it could just as well be done in steel or plastic or cardboard. The paint is here only to hide the material, not to change it, transform it, or add any other quality to it. Ultimately the balcony as an architectural element cannot express itself; it has no identity, no personality—it is downgraded to just being here and remaining here in its stupid ugliness. But the balcony is not quiet;

it doesn't remain still. On the contrary, it screams because it is profoundly unhappy with its dumb role. How does it scream? It does not send acoustic signals but visual, aesthetic ones. It makes the whole of the auditorium look stupid; it communicates how uninspired and disrespectful were the architects of that entire space.

Mori   This is an interesting comment on the fusion of technological developments and the raising of consciousness, and a desire to engage more with the world of spirituality. The power of materials is limitless, but it is enhanced by the consciousness of an architect, and the question is how to use that power. How do you give material character? How do you give it a narrative? As he says, the material is dumb—it won't do anything for you unless you approach it with conscious effort.

Herzog   Training the senses also plays a key role. If you don't use all of your five senses, some of them will atrophy while others, being overly stressed and used, will evolve in new ways. At the current stage of human civilization, most of our perceptional energy is absorbed

Herzog & de Meuron, Pfaffenholz Sports Center

by the visual impact of electronic media. Visual and acoustic signals seem to depend less on material structures than smell, taste, or touch. In other words, our culture leans toward more immaterial values than did previous periods. This process may be enhanced by prosthetic electronic tools that can be implanted to improve all kinds of human performance. Genetic engineering may even produce human beings whose perceptional capacities will reach beyond the five senses that evolution has developed so far.

Mori I hope not! (laughter)

Herzog What I want to say is that we live in a moment of human history where many things that seemed to be eternal givens are suddenly subject to dramatic change. The globalization of the markets, the electronic media, biotechnology, and genetic engineering have had and will continue to have an influence on our human condition. One example is—as I stated before—the impact on our five senses and therefore on our perception of the world. This is not

something that we wish to celebrate but rather something that Herzog and de Meuron has always given a lot of attention to. Our work has always been conceived to appeal to all five senses, consciously involving also tactile issues and even smell. This clearly demonstrates that we believe in an architecture that stresses its material and physical conditions to perform successfully, in conscious contrast to an architecture based on illustration and imagery, such as Disney World. And as I said at the beginning, there is a paradox in this affirmation of the material aspect of architecture, because ultimately it is the moment when materiality transcends into immateriality that we are after. To achieve this transcendence, or to put it more modestly, this moment of understanding —of public acceptance in the case of big urban projects—we often use a strategy of hypermateriality, a strategy where the material conditions of the structure in the making are involved from the very beginning.

Mori One way in which architects are described is that we know a little about a lot of things. And that model has worked well. If we go back 200 years, when we worked

81

Herzog & de Meuron, Ricola-Europe SA, Production and Storage Building

with people specializing in craft, we were able to rely on their knowledge of materials and the fairly limited palette of materials that existed. But that craft knowledge is being lost quickly, and therefore our connection to materials is also disappearing. The other aspect is that we are seeing a proliferation of new materials, from varied fields and practically on a daily basis, which we don't necessarily understand. Can you talk a little more about the process and how you gather knowledge of an actual material? How do you develop —I don't want to say a craft sense for the material, but the kind of works and explorations, and modes of representation, that you go through. For example, for Prada, how did

you develop that idea for fiberglass? Do you actually have a lab? And what limitations are imposed on how much knowledge you can generate, because you are taking on a lot of new responsibilities?

Herzog How do we develop new materials, how does research in an architectural practice function? It's really rather primitive. Of course we do have a professional workshop integrated in our Basel offices. But we don't have our own media lab or someone who is permanently busy with material research independently from a project. Our experience is very much based on the concrete reality of a project and on trial-and-error as a method of research. For Prada Tokyo, we were experimenting with all kinds of fiberglass and its translucent qualities. We used glass

fibers and tested different ways to diffuse the light. We finally integrated them into fiberglass and activated them electrically. The result is an independently luminous, almost skinlike membrane. The whole thing is new in its combination of fibers, even if the single products have been on the market for a long time, so we decided to work on a patent for it. That discovery was a side effect of our research for new display furniture for Prada. In a similar way we tested things for the Dominus Winery to achieve heavy stone walls with a paradoxical capacity to breathe, to be porous and see-through. And that's how we ended up discovering multiple ways to use steel gabions.

Mori One of the things that we advocate is to actively seek industry collaboration and support, and try to see if the industry will sponsor the next phase of research. If you do material research in academia, the information is available to everybody, whereas when it is privatized, it becomes some company's private property. It then becomes very expensive and therefore unusable. What do you feel about the proprietary nature of material research in architecture?

Herzog Copyrights and patents are a possible way to protect your private research. We are currently patenting the kind of fiberglass I was describing before. It is a very delicate and expensive business, and nobody knows if you will ever get back the money you invested in both the research and the legal fees for the patenting. Your patent may be protected in one country but not in all countries. Where do you protect it, who takes care of all those copyright issues? Do you build a new company for that, or should it be an integral part of your design company? All these questions are very complex and only later, maybe years later, will you know which path would have been the

right one. One example where we clearly were too naive and missed a chance to protect our research was the photochemical treatment of concrete surfaces that we used for the Eberswalde Library. Technically the process already existed, but it had never been used to combine photography and concrete. That was absolutely new and opened up doors for interesting applications as well as for the worst kitsch. Unfortunately, it has been copied numerous times for dumb commercial projects, namely in France and Germany. Of course we never got any money from these imitators.

Ron Witte I was wondering if you would comment on the difference between trying to extract the material's intrinsic quality and the imposition of quality on material? I don't mean to suggest that that's the right characterization of your work. But could you compare the extraction of certain qualities from the skin of the signal box, versus the imposition of a condition in the case of, say, Ricola?

Herzog Yes, you might speak of extraction versus imposition. You could also try to find other names for the process of transforming and using materials, but

that is not so important. In the case of Ricola Mulhouse, where we used silkscreen printing on ordinary industrial polycarbonate slabs, you can speak of a more active process of transformation. You call it "imposition," but one could also call it "inscription," tattooing, which expresses something physical, something you relate to your body. The copper-clad signal boxes use a traditional building material, but apply it in a new way. The twisting copper bands running around the building express their inherent material qualities in a very radical and straightforward way. They are what they are. Here you can speak of a more passive, less aggressive way to interfere in the "genetic code" of the material.

Marco Steinberg In certain Swiss traditions, the use of material has been in a way a search for truth—indigenous materials used in a truthful way. Frequently wood will be without paint, for example. And there is an expression of the truth of the material in itself. There's a distinction between the appearance of something and what is actually there. The material may appear to be doing certain things, yet there is a relationship behind the scenes.

83

For example, removing emollients seems like a simple act, yet somehow the glass becomes pure, or maybe it is more truthful. But what is your relationship then to overcome the things that actually might not be visible?

Herzog   Like I said before: there are more active and more passive ways to interfere in the world of materials. Painting wood or exposing it nakedly are just two possible ways to use that material. Both ways can be right or wrong, true or untrue, or whatever. Nothing is real or right or correct in itself; it may be so because it's part of a system or a concept where things begin to interact together. You can find examples of a more active or a rather passive attitude toward the transformation of matter way back in the history of human cultures.

Tala Klinck   I wonder whether you could talk about scale and how you experience, in particular, your facades—both from far away and up close—and how this determines your manipulation of materials.

Herzog   Any distance, any moment of scale, can be right. Take a printed photograph, which is built on a pixel structure. It can be quite intriguing to look at the pixel structure as a reality in its own right, in contrast to a distant look at the same image, where you no longer see the grain and it is just the overall image. How you deal with these different moments and distances and scales is one important issue in architecture, and in human perception.

Audience   With your buildings, it is hard to visualize where the builders start, and when you stop. Is there a collaborative building process? Or are you becoming the builder again?

Herzog   No, certainly not. The tendency is for the architect to disappear from the site. There are different models. Of course we try to control a building as much as we can. There are large-scale projects like the soccer stadium in Basel where, from the start, we knew that we would not be able to control the whole design, so we built our design strategy on four very strong concepts that we tried to strictly control: one for the shape of the building, one for the interior space, one for the colors, and another one for the luminosity of the facades. But even there, the detailing was

sometimes so lousy that there was a question of whether we should keep that commission instead of stepping down as designers. We decided to stay because we wanted to realize that building, which has now become so important for the people in Basel who are enthusiastic soccer fans. But we learned an important lesson: there are different scales in your work, and sometimes your design survives only if you base it on a solid and simple design strategy, which you have to communicate from the beginning. Decide early what makes sense for you to control. That requires quite a lot of experience, of course, but it's very important. If you fight for every single nail, you lose. And sometimes a designer doesn't need that, if the project as a whole works and makes sense. The situation must be similar if you do an airport or a big train station.

Mori   The Tate is a good example of a large project where you strategized in a different way.

Herzog   The Tate is completely different, a highly prestigious cultural project, where we had to control every single thing. But in the UK there is a big gap between builders

84

Herzog & de Meuron, Dominus Winery

and architects, so we tested everything with mockups. And most
of the things were built like the
mockups, but not everything, so
that was also quite a struggle. And
of course we couldn't redo every
single part of the building, so we
needed to make strict, clear-cut
decisions. Some of the things were
detailed and built with extreme
refinement, while others we left
almost brutally raw. Sometimes
you can make that clear distinction
because it is obvious that an architect cannot play the same role

that the craftsman played in earlier
times. But we shouldn't become
cynical and say, well, I don't care
anymore, or I just don't accept
large-scale commercial projects
anymore. Because, even if you have
limited influence on a large-scale
project, if you choose the right
strategies, it can make a huge difference, and it is very important
that these extra-large projects are
not left to anonymous builders
and developers.

Albrecht, Donald, ed. *The Work of Charles and Ray Eames: A Legacy of Invention*. New York: Harry N. Abrams in association with the Library of Congress, 1997.

Amato, Ivan. *Stuff: The Material the World Is Made Of*. New York: Basic Books, 1997.

Antonelli, Paola. *Mutant Materials in Contemporary Design*. New York: Museum of Modern Art, 1995.

Baird, George. *The Space of Appearance*. Cambridge, MA: MIT Press, 1995.

Ball, Philip. *Made to Measure: New Materials for the Twenty-first Century*. Princeton, N.J.: Princeton University Press, 1997.

Behne, Adolf. "Art, Craft, Technology." *Figures of Architecture and Thought: German Architecture Culture, 1880–1920*. Edited by Francesco Dal Co. New York: Rizzoli, 1990.

Banham, Rayner. *The Architecture of the Well-Tempered Environment*. 2d ed. Chicago: University of Chicago Press, 1984.

Banham, Rayner. *Theory and Design in the First Machine Age*. 2d ed. New York: Praeger, 1970.

Beukers, Adriaan, and Ed van Hinte. *Lightness: The Inevitable Renaissance of Minimum Energy Structures*. Rotterdam: 010 Publishers, 1998.

Bois, Yves Alain, and Rosalind E. Krauss. *Formless: A User's Guide*. New York: Zone Books, 1997.

Calvino, Italo. *Six Memos for the Next Millennium*. The Charles Eliot Norton Lectures; 1985–86. Cambridge, MA: Harvard University Press, 1988.

Candilis, G., Blomstedt, T. Frangoulis, and M.I. Amorin. *Bugholzmobel: Muebles en Bois Courbe/Bent Wood Furniture*. Stuttgart: Karl Kramer Verlag, 1979.

Chandler, Maurice Henry. *Ceramics in the Modern World: Man's First Technology Comes of Age*. Garden City, N.Y.: Doubleday, 1968.

Cutcliffe, Stephen H., and Terry S. Reynolds, eds. *Technology and American History: A Historical Anthology from Technology and Culture*. Chicago: University of Chicago Press, 1997.

Diderot, Denis. *A Diderot Pictorial Encyclopedia of Trades and Industry: Manufacturing and the Technical Arts in Plates Selected from "L'encyclopedie, ou Dictionnaire Raisonné des Sciences, des Arts, et des Metiers."* Edited by Charles Coulston Gillispie. Dover, 1959.

Dreyfuss, Henry. *Designing for People*. New York: Simon and Schuster, 1955.

Drexler, Arthur. *Charles Eames: Furniture from the Design Collection, The Museum of Modern Art, New York*. New York: Museum of Modern Art, 1973.

El-Khoury, Rudolph. "Polish and Deodorize: Paving the City in Late Eighteenth-Century France." *Assemblage* 31 (1996): 6–15.

selected readings

Engen, Trygg. *Odor Sensation and Memory*. New York: Praeger Press, 1991.

Ezrahi, Yaron, Everett Mendelsohn, and Howard Segal. *Technology, Pessimism, and Postmodernism*. Boston: Kluwer Academic Publishers, 1994.

Feenberg, Andrew. *Critical Theory of Technology*. New York: Oxford University Press, 1991.

Forty, Adrian. *Objects of Desire: Design and Society, 1750–1980*. New York: Pantheon Books, 1986.

Frampton, Kenneth. *Modern Architecture: A Critical History*. New York: Oxford University Press, 1980.

Frampton, Kenneth. *Studies in Tectonic Culture*. Cambridge, MA: Harvard University Graduate School of Design, 1985.

Frankel, Felice, and George M. Whiteside. *On the Surface of Things: Images of the Extraordinary in Science*. San Francisco: Chronicle Books, 1997.

Garner, Philippe. *Eileen Gray: Design and Architecture, 1878–1976*. Cologne: Taschen, 1993.

Giedion, Sigfried. *Mechanization Takes Command*. New York: Oxford University Press, 1948.

Gordon, J. E. *The New Science of Strong Materials: Or Why You Don't Fall Through the Floor*. 2d ed. Princeton, N.J.: Princeton University Press, 1984.

Habegger, Jerryll, and Joseph H. Osman. *Sourcebook of Modern Furniture*. 2d ed. New York: W.W. Norton, 1996.

Haynes, Williams. *Cellulose: The Chemical That Grows*. Garden City, NY: Doubleday, 1953.

Hickman, Larry A. *John Dewey's Pragmatic Technology*. Bloomington: Indiana University Press, 1990.

Huyssen, Andreas. "The Hidden Dialectic: Avant-garde—Technology—Mass Culture." *After the Great Divide: Modernism, Mass Culture, Postmodernism*. Bloomington: Indiana University Press, 1986.

Illich, Ivan. H_2O *and the Waters of Forgetfulness*. London: Boyars, 1986.

Kauffman, Stuart. *At Home in the Universe: The Search for Laws of Self-Organization and Complexity*. New York: Oxford University Press, 1995.

Kipnis, Jeffrey. "The Cunning of Cosmetics." *El Croquis* 84 (1997): 22–28.

Kirkham, Pat. *Charles and Ray Eames: Designers of the Twentieth Century*. Cambridge, MA: MIT Press, 1995.

Kwinter, Sanford. "Architecture and the Technologies of Life." *AA Files*, no. 27 (1994): 3–4.

Levenson, Thomas. "How Not to Make a Stradivarius." *American Scholar* 53 (1994): 351–378.

Loos, Adolf. *Spoken into the Void: Collected Essays, 1897–1900.* Translated by Jane O. Newman and John H. Smith. Cambridge, MA: MIT Press, 1982.

Martinez, Enrique, and Marco Steinberg, eds. *Material Legacies: Bamboo.* Providence: Department of Industrial Design, Rhode Island School of Design, 2000.

Maxwell, Robert. "Positive Futures: The Lure of Technology." *The Two-Way Stretch: Modernism, Tradition, and Innovation.* London: Academy Editions, 1996.

McLuhan, Marshall. *Understanding Media: The Extensions of Man.* New York: McGraw-Hill, 1966.

Materials: A Scientific American Book. San Francisco: W. H. Freeman, 1967.

McCarty, Cara, and Matilda McQuaid. *Structure and Surface: Contemporary Japanese Textiles.* New York: Museum of Modern Art, 1998.

Meikle, Jeffrey. *American Plastic: A Cultural History.* New Brunswick, N.J.: Rutgers University Press, 1995.

Mumford, Lewis. *Technics and Civilization.* New York: Harcourt, Brace, and Company, 1934.

Museum of Finnish Architecture, Finnish Society of Crafts and Design. *Alvar Aalto Furniture.* Cambridge, MA: MIT Press, 1985.

Neumeyer, Fritz. *The Artless Word: Mies Van der Rohe on the Building Art.* Cambridge, MA: MIT Press, 1991.

Negroponte, Nicholas. *Being Digital.* New York: Knopf, 1995.

Neuhart, John, Marilyn Newhart, and Ray Eames. *Eames Design: The Work of the Office of Charles and Ray Eames.* New York: Harry N. Abrams, 1989.

Neutra, Richard. "The Sound and Smell of Architecture." *Progressive Architecture,* no. 30 (November 1949): 65–66.

Nye, David E. *American Technological Sublime.* Cambridge, MA: MIT Press, 1996.

Pallasmaa, Juhani. *The Eyes of the Skin: Architecture and the Senses.* London: Academy Editions, 1996.

Pallasmaa, Juhani. "Hapticity and Time: Notes on a Fragile Architecture." *The Architectural Review* 207, no. 1239 (May 2000): 78–84.

Perry, Thomas D. *Modern Plywood.* 2d ed. New York: Pitman, 1948.

Peters, Tom F. *Building the Nineteenth Century.* Cambridge, MA: MIT Press, 1996.

Perez-Gomez, Alberto. *Architecture and the Crisis of Modern Science.* Cambridge, MA: MIT Press, 1983.

Phillips, Charles John. *Glass: The Miracle Maker, Its History, Technology, and Applications.* New York: Pitman, 1941.

Picon, Antoine. "Towards a History of Technological Thought." *Technological Change—Methods and Themes in the History of Technology*. Edited by Robert Fox. London: Harwood Academic Publishers, 1996.

Pina, Leslie. *Fifties Furniture*. Atglen, PA: Schiffer, 1996.

Pine, Joseph B. *Mass Customization: The New Frontier in Business Competition*. Boston: Harvard Business School Press, 1993.

Pippin, Robert. "On the Notion of Technology as Ideology: Prospects." *Technology, Pessimism, and Postmodernism*. Edited by Yaron Ezrahi, Everett Mendelsohn, and Howard Segal. Amherst: University of Massachusetts Press, 1995.

Rieman, Timothy D., and Jean M. Burks. *The Complete Book of Shaker Furniture*. New York: Harry N. Abrams, 1993.

Robinson, Clark Norval. *Meet the Plastics*. New York: Macmillan, 1949.

Rykwert, Joseph. *The Dancing Column: On the Orders of Architecture*. Cambridge, MA: MIT Press, 1996.

Schumacher, E. F. *Small Is Beautiful*. London: Blond and Briggs, 1973.

Simon, Joan. "Miyake Modern." *Art in America* 87, no. 2 (February 1999): 78–83.

Sparke, Penny, ed. *The Plastics Age: From Bakelite to Beanbags and Beyond*. Woodstock, N.Y.: Overlook Press, 1993.

Steinberg, Marco. *Prototype for a Plywood Wheelchair*. Cambridge, MA: Harvard University Graduate School of Design, 1999.

Taylor, Frederick Winslow. *The Principles of Scientific Management*. New York: Norton, 1947.

Thonet, Gebruder. *Thonet Bentwood and Other Furniture: The 1904 Illustrated Catalogue*. New York: Dover, 1980.

Tschumi, Bernard. *Architecture and Disjunction*. Cambridge, MA: MIT Press, 1998.

Tschumi, Bernard. "Architecture and Transgression." *Oppositions Reader*. Edited by K. Michael Hays. New York: Princeton Architectural Press, 1998.

Vegesack, Alexander von. *Thonet: Classic Furniture in Bent Wood and Tubular Steel*. New York: Rizzoli, 1997.

Vroon, Piet. *Smell: The Secret Seducer*. Translated by Paul Vincent. New York: Farrar, Straus, and Giroux, 1997.

Witte, Ron, ed. *CASE: Toyo Ito / Sendai Mediatheque*. Munich: Prestel, 2002.

Mette Aamodt is a graduate student in the MArch I program at the Harvard Design School.

Ivan Amato is a freelance writer specializing in science and technology issues and an editor of the weekly magazine *Science News*. He also explores less conventional means of examining and communicating these issues in media ranging from poetry to puppetry. Amato is currently working on a book of science imagery to be published by Harry Abrams in 2003.

Shigeru Ban is the principal of Shigeru Ban Architects in Tokyo. He is also a Professor of Architecture at Keio University, Tokyo. He was awarded, among numerous prizes, the World Architecture Award 2001, European Category, for the Japan Pavilion at the Hannover Expo. A book about Ban's work was published by Princeton Architectural Press.

James Carpenter is the principal of James Carpenter Design Associates, a design collaborative that explores the natural phenomena of light through the development of new glass and material technologies. He is a visiting professor at the University of Stuttgart's Lightweight Structures Institute. Carpenter was a visiting professor in the Department of Materials Science and Engineering at MIT in spring 2000, and he was the Eliot Noyes Visiting Professor at the Harvard Design School in fall of that year. He was also a Loeb Fellow at the School in 1989. He received, among other awards, the first-place prize from the Illuminating Engineering Society for "Light Threshold," a project for the 2000 Sydney Olympics.

Michael Cima is the Sumitomo Electric Industries Professor in the Department of Materials Science and Engineering at MIT. He is also the director of the Ceramics Processing Research Laboratory. Cima is the winner of the International Award of Materials Engineering for Resources in 1998. He is the co-principal investigator on MIT's innovative 3D printing process for rapid prototyping of components from powder materials.

contributors

Merrill Elam is a principal of Mack Scogin Merrill Elam Architects, Inc., in Atlanta, Georgia. She was a visiting critic at both the Harvard Design School and SCI-Arc. Elam was also the Louis Henry Sullivan Research Professor of Architecture at the University of Illinois at Chicago, the William Henry Bishop Visiting Professor at Yale University, and the Harry S. Shure Visiting Professor in Architecture at the University of Virginia. She is the recipient of an academy award in architecture from the American Academy of Arts and Letters, and she received the Chrysler Award in 1996. Her publications include Rizzoli's *Scogin Elam and Bray: Critical Architecture/Architectural Criticism* and *Mack and Merrill,* published by the University of Michigan.

Kristen Giannattasio is a 2001 MArch I graduate of the Harvard Design School.

Laurie Hawkinson is a principal of Smith-Miller + Hawkinson Architects of New York City. She is an Associate Professor at the Columbia University Graduate School of Architecture, Planning, and Preservation. Her recent publication is *Between Spaces: Smith-Miller + Hawkinson Architecture, Judith Turner Photography.*

Jacques Herzog is a principal of Herzog & de Meuron in Basel, Switzerland. He is the Arthur Roach Design Critic in Architecture at the Harvard Design School. He was the winner of the Pritzker Architecture Prize in 2001 along with his partner, Pierre de Meuron.

Sheila Kennedy is a principal of Kennedy & Violich Architecture in Boston. As an Associate Professor at the Harvard Design School, she published *Bugs, Fish, Floors, and Ceilings: Luminous Bodies and the Contemporary Problem of Material Presence.* Her recent publication is *Material Misuse,* published by the Architectural Association of London.

Tala Klinck is a graduate student in the MArch I program at the Harvard Design School.

Hiroto Kobayashi is an architect. He has worked for Norman Foster and Nikken Sekkei and is presently researching Japanese urban forms as a doctoral student at the Harvard Design School.

Richard Lee is a 2001 MAUD graduate of the Harvard Design School.

John May is a graduate student in the MArch I program at the Harvard Design School.

Toshiko Mori is the Robert P. Hubbard Professor in the Practice of Architecture at the Harvard Design School and chair of the Department of Architecture. She is also the principal of Toshiko Mori Architect of New York City. Her research and practice involve innovative use of traditional and new materials and exploration of alternative fabrication methods for architecture and design.

Mark Mulligan teaches courses in building technology at the Harvard Design School, focusing on the relationship between design, detail, and construction. He has written and translated published essays on contemporary Japanese architectural practice and has lectured on this subject in the United States and abroad.

Dan Schodek is Kumagai Professor of Architectural Technology at the Harvard Design School. He is a specialist in building technology as it relates to architectural design. The author of several books, Schodek has most recently pursued research in the development of construction applications of computer-aided manufacturing techniques.

92

Mack Scogin is a principal in the firm of Mack Scogin Merrill Elam Architects, Inc., in Atlanta, Georgia. He is the Kajima Adjunct Professor of Architecture at the Harvard Design School, where he was chair of the department of architecture from 1990 to 1995. He received the 1995 academy award in architecture from the American Academy of Arts and Letters, and he was the recipient of the Chrysler Award in 1996. The work of Scogin and Elam is the subject of the Rizzoli publication *Scogin Elam and Bray: Critical Architecture /Architectural Criticism* and *Mack and Merrill*, published by the University of Michigan.

Marco Steinberg is an architect practicing in Finland and the United States. Steinberg is an Associate Professor of Architecture at the Harvard Design School, where he teaches design studios and seminars on product design, materials, and fabrication technologies. He has also taught architecture and product design at the Rhode Island School of Design.

Nader Tehrani is a founding partner of Office dA in Boston. Tehrani is an Adjunct Associate Professor of Architecture at the Harvard Design School, where he teaches design studios and seminars on new technologies. He has also taught architecture at Northeastern University and the Rhode Island School of Design.

Shozo Toyohisa calls himself a lighting architect. His work ranges from urban projects to museum lighting. He invents lighting systems and designs lighting equipment and fixtures that are unique to each project. His has a master's degree in material science and worked as an award-winning industrial designer; his work is in the collection of the Metropolitan Museum, MoMA, and the Canadian National Museum. Among numerous awards, he has received the Silver Medal of the Art Directors' Club of New York for his lighting installation at MoMA.

Heather Walls is a 2001 MArch I graduate of the Harvard Design School.

Ean White is a nationally recognized artist who works with sound performance and installation, video, lighting, and pyrotechnics. Based in Boston, he occasionally conducts workshops and lectures at area colleges and is currently studio manager at Harvard University's Studio for Electroacoustic Composition.

Ron Witte is an architect. He is a founding partner of WW in Cambridge, Massachusetts. Witte is also an Associate Professor of Architecture at the Harvard School of Design, where he teaches design studios and seminars on new technologies.

Illustration Credits

Illustrations courtesy Harvard Design School: cover (Dan Bibb), ii, vi, xiv (Paul Warchol), 2, 3, 4 (upper left and right by Paul Warchol), 5, 6, 7 (left by Paul Warchol), 22, 24, 25, 26, 27 (Paul Warchol), 40, 42, 44, 45, 46–47 (Paul Warchol), 62, 64 (Paul Warchol), 66, 67, 69 (right by Paul Warchol), 70, 72, 73, 74 (Paul Warchol). Photos courtesy Mack Scogin Merrill Elam Architects: 8 (Timothy Hursley), 9. Photos courtesy Kennedy & Violich Architecture: 10, 14 (Bruce T. Martin), 15. Photos courtesy Smith-Miller + Hawkinson Architects: 16 (Robert Polodori), 17 (Michael Moran), 18 (Paul Warchol). Photos courtesy Shigeru Ban Architects (Hiroyuki Hirai): 28, 29, 30, 31, 32, 35. Photos courtesy James Carpenter Design Associates: 48, 51, 52, 57. Photo courtesy Shozo Toyohisa (Harunobu Izumo): 77. Photos courtesy Herzog & de Meuron: 78, 79, 81, 82, 85.